⟨ **W9-AOH-542**

J
07/17

Nurturing Next-Generation Innovators

Open-Ended Activities to Support Global Thinking

by Ellen Booth Church

Nurturing Next-Generation Innovators

Open-Ended Activities to Support Global Thinking

by Ellen Booth Church

Gryphon House
www.gryphonhouse.com

WEST HARTFORD
PUBLIC LIBRARY
8071

Copyright
©2016 Ellen Booth Church

Published by Gryphon House, Inc.
P. O. Box 10, Lewisville, NC 27023
800.638.0928; 877.638.7576 (fax)
Visit us on the web at www.gryphonhouse.com.

All rights reserved. No part of this publication may be reproduced or transmitted in any form or by any means, electronic or technical, including photocopy, recording, or any information storage or retrieval system, without prior written permission of the publisher. Printed in the United States. Every effort has been made to locate copyright and permission information.
Cover and interior photographs used under license from Shutterstock.com.

Library of Congress Cataloging-in-Publication Data
The Cataloging-in-Publication Data is registered with the Library of Congress for ISBN 978-0-87659-668-5.

Bulk Purchase
Gryphon House books are available for special premiums and sales promotions as well as for fund-raising use. Special editions or book excerpts also can be created to specifications. For details, call 800.638.0928.

Disclaimer
Gryphon House, Inc., cannot be held responsible for damage, mishap, or injury incurred during the use of or because of activities in this book. Appropriate and reasonable caution and adult supervision of children involved in activities and corresponding to the age and capability of each child involved are recommended at all times. Do not leave children unattended at any time. Observe safety and caution at all times.

J
370.116
CHURCH

Dedication

To my grandmother, Francesca Esterly Korn, and the many generations of creative and innovative thinkers in my family. Thank you for teaching me that anything is possible.

And to my creative husband, Jerry Levine, who makes everything possible.

Table of Contents

Preface ix

Introduction 1
    How to Use This Book 3

An Open-Ended Approach to Learning 5
    Global Guidelines and Key Philosophies 7
    The Change in Play 8
    The Importance of Hands-On Experiences 9
    The Necessity of Making Mistakes—Developing a Growth Mindset . . . 11
    The Art and Wisdom of Problem Solving 12
    Skills for Exploring Learning Themes 12
    Communicating with Families 15

Theme One: How I See the World—The Art of Observing and Comparing . . . 19
    Playing with Names 20
    Playing with the Letters of My Name 23
    Playing with Lines 26
    Playing with Sounds 29
    Playing with Opposites 32
    My Face, Your Face 34
    My Body, Your Body 37
    How My Body Works 41
    My Sense of Seeing 44
    Seeing with All My Senses 47

Theme Two: How I Interact with the World—Understanding the Needs and
    Feelings of Ourselves and Others 51
    I Am, You Are 52
    So Many Messages 55
    Puppets Speak! 58
    Communicating without Words 60
    Who Needs Me, and How Can I Help? 62
    Every Living Thing Needs Water 66
    We All Need a Place to Live 69
    We All Need to Feel Safe and Healthy 72
    Everybody Needs to Eat 75
    Animals Have Needs, Too! 79

Theme Three: How I Live in the World—Playing and Working Together 83
   It's All Child's Play and Work 84
   Work and Play in the Community. 87
   Our Family Works and Plays Together 90
   Problem Solving with Work and Play 93
   We Can Follow Directions. 97
   That's Funny!. 100
   Tools Help Us Work and Play 103
   Energy Helps Us Work and Play 107
   Cooking with Tools and Energy 110
   Playing and Working with Light and Shadow 113

Theme Four: How I Experience the World—Everything Changes 117
   What Is Change?. 118
   Weather Changes 121
   What's in a Season? 124
   What Time Is It Now?. 127
   Seeds Become Plants. 131
   Cooking and Changing Food 135
   Animals Grow and Change, Too! 138
   I Can Make Changes 141
   Growing Up 144
   Then and Now. 148

References and Recommended Reading 153

Index 155

Preface

I have been working with and for young children since 1971. Whether as a preschool or kinder-garten teacher or as a college instructor working with future teachers, my heart and mind have been focused on helping children to love learning and to live and thrive in the world that is ahead for them. This can be challenging because we often don't know what is ahead for children. In my keynote speeches around the world, I often ask the audience to pause and think about what the world might be like when the young children they are now teaching are their age or even my age. We discuss many ideas, often related to technology and society. The one conclusion we always come to is that the only constant is change.

Everything changes, and it seems to each generation that change happens very quickly. My father was born in 1896 and traveled in a covered wagon as a child. Before he passed away at age ninety, humans had landed on the moon. That is a great deal of change. Think about your own life and the changes that have happened to date. I wrote my first book in 1983, in longhand because I didn't know how to type. Now, I am sitting at my computer writing to you as I look at the birds on the feeder outside the window. I don't even need to look at my hands or the screen. That is a huge change for me!

I invite you to pause right now. Put down this book, and look out your window. Imagine the chil-dren you teach. What do you think the world will be like when they are your age? What skills will they need? What challenges and gifts will they deal with? How can you prepare them for a future of change?

Please join me on a journey through creative themes chosen to support children's global view and understanding. Enjoy these activities that are designed to support children as they develop into global thinkers, communicators, and collaborators. I promise you, it will be fun along the way.

—Ellen Booth Church

Introduction

The mediocre teacher tells. The good teacher explains. The superior teacher demonstrates. The great teacher inspires.

—William Arthur Ward, author

Children who are prepared to deal with the world of work and education need to be able to take a broad view. What does this mean? It means being able to see many viewpoints and perspectives. It also means being able to listen to others and to share one's own ideas and perceptions.

Think about perspective and perception. There are two very interesting and important processes we can introduce to start preparing children for the wide world ahead. First, we present children with activities that invite them to take many different perspectives. Then, from those viewpoints, we encourage them to notice what they perceive. The themes in this book are meant to ask children to broaden their perspectives, to notice relationships, to investigate same and different, to use perception to develop inductive and deductive reasoning, and to evaluate their processes and thinking. That all might sound like big stuff for young children, but when it is presented with fun songs, games, and activities, nothing is more natural!

This book is designed differently from traditional activity books where the sections are divided by skill or curriculum area. When we operate in the world, we don't separate the skills. Instead, we use them all together for success and understanding. This book is divided into four major themes that walk children through ever-increasing understandings of their place in the wide world ahead. Literacy, math, science, motor, and social skills are woven into each theme so that the children's experience is well-rounded, both socially and intellectually.

The goal of this book is to provide teachers with creative hands-on discussions and activities for developing children who are thinkers, communicators, and collaborators. Just as we are asking children to be both creative and critical thinkers, this book also is asking you to be a creative, critical thinker. Each activity is full of ideas and inspirations to use with the children. Treat this book like a menu at your favorite restaurant—choose the items that fit your classroom "appetite" right now. You can always revisit the menu another time and try something new!

How do we prepare children to thrive in the ever-changing global community? We teach them:

- To observe and notice.
- To relate to their own needs and the needs of others.
- To work and play well with others.
- To recognize and even love change.
- To thrive in a changing world.

How do we do prepare children for the unexpected, the changing dynamics of life?

- We offer them hands-on experiences with real-world materials.
- We support them in using problem-solving and thinking skills.
- We encourage them to share their thinking with others.
- We listen to their ideas and ask questions to take them further.
- We create a supportive classroom community of equals.

Theme One: How I See the World—The Art of Observing and Comparing

This theme focuses on building the thinking processes needed to compare, observe, discriminate, classify, and name what we see in the world around us. How are we the same and different? What do we notice in the world around us—color, shape, size, the five senses? The children will design critical and creative innovations to apply these understandings.

Theme Two: How I Interact with the World—Understanding the Needs and Feelings of Ourselves and Others

This theme focuses on a child's inner and outer worlds and the cognitive and affective skills needed to succeed. What do I need? What do others need? What do plants and animals need? How do I feel? How do I help others? The children will begin to learn to recognize the needs and feelings of the creatures in the world around us. They will create innovations for communicating and making connections.

Theme Three: How I Live in the World—Playing and Working Together

This theme focuses on taking the understanding out into the external world by exploring the way children and others process work and play. How do things work? What tools do we use?

How does my family work and play? What is my work? Children will explore work and play, tools and machines, working with energy, and light and shadow. They will begin thinking about taking on challenges and self-directed learning.

Theme Four: How I Experience the World—Everything Changes

This theme focuses on exploring and understanding the life processes within children and the world around them. How do I grow and change? What do I notice about the changes around me? What are short-term and long-term changes? How do I make change happen? The children will begin to take perspectives and develop self-control and focus.

> *I never teach my pupils; I only attempt to provide the conditions in which they can learn.*
>
> —Albert Einstein, physicist

How to Use This Book

We want children to look at the world ahead with perspective and perception. Part of the design of this book is to invite you to examine familiar curriculum topics with new eyes. Being ready for the global community means having the ability to look at things from different points of view. As you move through these activities that at first might seem familiar, be prepared to view them in new ways with a global perspective of inclusion and creativity.

Each theme is divided into ten topics. Each topic has enough circle-time, exploration-time, and extension-time activities to last many days. You know your group better than anybody, so please feel free to choose, mix, and match the activities any way you like. That gives you more than fifty weeks of activities to experiment with. While there is no set way to work with the activities, here is a simple formula to keep in mind:

- **Introduce the activity.** Instead of telling children what the activity is, give them clues to engage problem-solving and thinking. Sing a song, play a game—do anything that will get them wondering about the topic. It is always good to start with a song that has a familiar tune that children can follow.

- **Show the materials and talk about them.** Consider asking children to brainstorm about the materials or the concept you are introducing. Be open to their creative ideas.

- **Invite children to join small groups for in-depth explorations.** Most of the activities are best suited for groups of five or six children. These can be done during your center time so that the rest of the children are easily occupied in other areas while you work with the small group.

If we look ahead to the future, this might be what we see: Children who can see the world with new eyes, work with the world with care and commitment, live in the world with compassion and confidence, experience the world of growth and change with skill and understanding.

- **Get children started, and then step back.** Once a group is happily working on a project, you can move around the room to see what other groups are doing. Ask questions, start conversations, and support thinking.

- **Encourage children to suggest variations and extensions on the original activities.** Often their ideas are the best!

TIP: Use Images to Bring the Wide World into the Classroom

Photos are a great way to bring the outside in. You will notice that many of the activities suggest that you provide children with magazines to cut for images. Look for a variety of magazines beyond the usual. Science and nature magazines are helpful. So are tool catalogs and magazines. Libraries often give away collections of outdated magazines. Ask parents to share their old magazines with you, too. Consider also searching online for photos to show the children. You can find wonderfully specific images to fit your topic of study. (Of course, you will want to observe all applicable copyright laws.)

An Open-Ended Approach to Learning

Everyone is a genius. But if you judge a fish on its ability to climb a tree, it will live its whole life believing that it is stupid.

—Albert Einstein (attributed)

Global education is not one-size-fits-all education. It is an approach to working with children that recognizes their individual strengths, interests, and abilities. There is no right or wrong way to do the activities in these themes. There may be suggested steps to presenting them, but the children should explore the topic in their own way and with their own thinking.

As you read the activities, you will notice an interesting blend of teacher-initiated and child-initiated ones. There are educational benefits to both types. An optimal program creates a balance by providing teacher-directed introductory activities—called Let's Get Inspired in this book—which spark children to take the topic in their own directions. By starting with your introduction, you know the children have the information and the basic skills needed to work independently. Of course, the more open-ended you are in your presentation, the more children will feel a sense of ownership in the process and will be inspired to explore further.

Teacher-initiated activities—called Let's Go!—introduce an idea, material, or process. But even in these activities, there is always time to stand back and allow children to work independently. Child-initiated activities inspire children to think by taking their own interests and ways of approaching something and applying them to a material or activity. Enjoy the blend in this book, and always look for a way to add both elements together in whatever you do with children. You will be creating the dynamic balance of content and experience that is at the core of individualized early childhood teaching.

It is important for children to feel recognized for their gifts. We do that by creating open-ended activities that meet children where they are and take them from there. Not everyone's idea will be the same, and that is a good thing! Accept all children's ideas equally. What might seem like a crazy idea could actually be brilliant. I will never forget when I realized this in my preschool class. I asked children to predict what we would see on our trip to the fire station. I wrote their ideas down on chart paper and accepted all ideas equally, even when little Julian said we would see a swimming pool at the fire station. Many adults would have told him no right from the beginning, but I wrote down swimming pool along with all the other ideas. When we got back from the trip, we revisited the chart. Sure enough, we had seen most of the things the children predicted, except a swimming pool. I asked Julian what he was thinking when he suggested we would see one at the fire station, and he answered loud and clear, "Well, they have to get the water from some- where, don't they?" His "wrong" answer was far from wrong. In fact, it opened us up to discussing where the water does come from!

> *No great discovery was ever made without a bold guess.*
>
> —Sir Isaac Newton, English mathematician and physicist

There is a great deal of concern among parents and teachers about children and their ability to compete in the ever-ex- panding global economy. We all ask the important questions that can set our intention for creative quality programs for children: How can we prepare children for a future in a world that is growing and changing so rapidly? What skills do they need to be successful? How can we nurture these skills natu- rally in children without pressuring them?

These big questions are at the core of child-centered and activity-based early childhood educa- tion. We might think that our preschool and kindergarten children are too young to think about a future that is so far away and vast. Yet, we also know that the opportunities we offer in the early years help children prepare for a future and for the world.

As teachers, we know the importance of developing children who know how to think creatively as well as critically. Inherent in this is the ability to face challenges with innovation and problem solving. How do children learn these skills?

- With hands-on, open-ended experiences that inspire as well as challenge.
- With opportunities to share an idea or a perspective without fear of being wrong.
- Within a supportive environment that celebrates diversity and creativity.

Life in the wide world ahead is not found on a workbook page. It is made of real objects and real problems. Children do not need to memorize facts as was the case years ago in education sys- tems. Now information is at their fingertips, and what is important is for children to know what to do with the information.

Daniel Pink, author of *A Whole New Mind: Why Right-Brainers Will Rule the Future*, suggests that our education system has evolved out of the Industrial Age of the nineteenth century, when there was a great need to memorize information and learn skills. He says that we have moved through the Information Age of the twentieth century and that we are now in the Conceptual Age, when creators, innovators, and "meaning makers" are needed to work with the challenges of this time. A key piece of functioning successfully is the ability to empathize with others' viewpoints and to solve problems on the spot together. He says, "In short, we've progressed from a society of farmers to a society of factory workers to a society of knowledge workers. And now we're progressing yet again—to a society of creators and empathizers, of pattern recognizers and meaning makers."

Global Guidelines and Key Philosophies

The Association for Childhood Education International (ACEI) recognizes the importance of creating global guidelines for early childhood education. Its guidelines reflect the importance of nurturing creative and innovative thinkers who know how to work together in a community. The "Global Guidelines for Early Childhood Education and Care in the 21st Century" were developed by a group of more than eighty international early care and education experts from twenty-seven countries. They address the fundamental elements necessary to create quality early care and education environments for young children around the world, and include the following:

> *Intelligence is the ability to adapt to change.*
>
> —Stephen Hawking, physicist

- Children are both the present and the future of every nation. They have needs, rights, and intrinsic worth that must be recognized and supported.

- Every child should have the opportunity to grow up in a setting that values children, that provides conditions for a safe and secure environment, and that respects diversity.

- Knowledge about human development is more substantial now than at any time in history. This century offers opportunities to consolidate recent gains and respond to new challenges that lie ahead.

- Children must receive appropriate nurture and education within and outside their families from birth onward if they are to develop optimally.

- Attention to the health, nutrition, education, and psychosocial development of children during their early years is essential for the future well-being of nations and the global community.

ACEI has also created a useful Global Guidelines Assessment (GGA) tool as part of their Global Guidelines. It can be downloaded at https://acei.org/news/acei-global-guidelines-assessment.

In her groundbreaking book *Minds in the Making,* Ellen Galinsky states that there are seven skills for success, which "involve weaving together our social, emotional, and intellectual capacities" that "begin to emerge during the preschool years." It is interesting to see how perfectly these seven skills represent good early childhood pedagogy. Spanning the range of social and cognitive areas of learning, Galinsky's suggested skills are embedded in the activities and themes of this book.

- Making connections
- Communication
- Focus and self-control
- Critical thinking

- Self-directed learning
- Perspective taking
- Taking on challenges

These seven skills are all inherent in play-based learning and are the essential elements to developing a balanced and competent child who is comfortable in the world. As you explore the activities in this book, you will find opportunities for children to develop these skills as well as the traditional skills of literacy, science, math, and so on.

The Change in Play

David Elkind, author of *The Power of Play: Learning What Comes Naturally,* wonders if play is being changed by the changes in the world. In his article "Can We Play?" written for the University of California at Berkeley website Greater Good: The Science of a Meaningful Life, he says:

> The decline of children's free, self-initiated play is the result of a perfect storm of technological innovation, rapid social change, and economic globalization.

> Technological innovations have led to the all-pervasiveness of television and computer screens in our society in general, and in our homes in particular. An unintended consequence of this invasion is that childhood has moved indoors. . .

> [A] global economy has increased parental fears about their children's prospects in an increasingly high-tech marketplace. . .

> Many middle-class parents have bought into the idea that education is a race, and that the earlier you start your child in academics, the better. . .

> We run the risk of pushing [children] into certain activities before they are ready, or stunting the development of important intellectual, social, or emotional skills. . .

> When we adults unite play, love, and work in our lives, we set an example that our children can follow. That just might be the best way to bring play back into the lives of our children—and build a more playful culture.

As you explore the themes and activities in this book, remember your role as playmate in addition to that of teacher. Your own playful approach to learning is both a model and an inspiration. None of the activities are set in stone. Perhaps one activity might make you think of another spinoff that fits you and the children. Or, maybe you want to adjust an activity to what you have on hand or who your group is. Do it. This is not a cookbook with recipes that must be followed to the letter. It is intended to inspire you and to encourage innovative education. When we are both flexible and responsive, we are building an education platform that is receptive to the wide world ahead.

As early childhood educators, we have always known the value of strong early learning programs. Recent studies have shown us even more about why these programs are so important. At the Education Nation Summit in 2011, researchers Patricia Kuhl and Andrew Meltzoff shared images of children's brains and demonstrated the importance of the first 2,000 days of a child's life for building synaptic connections in the billions of brain cells he is born with. During these early years, those brain cells get wired for use. We have the wonderful opportunity to work with these minds at this crucial time. By providing quality themes and activities presented in open-ended, real-life experiences, we can say we were part of the construction team in building the neural superhighways among those billions of brain cells!

> *Education is the most powerful weapon that you can use to change the world.*
> —Nelson Mandela, former president of South Africa, 1993 Nobel Peace Prize laureate

On First 2000 Days, the website of the North Carolina Early Childhood Foundation, Harvard pediatrician Jack Shonkoff refers to the studies that show that the brain is one of the few organs that are not fully developed at birth by saying, "Brains are built, not born." Shonkoff points out that the cells are there, but the wiring that forms the architecture is not. These connections are made through play-based activities and social interaction. He states, "Experiences and environments determine which connections get used more and, therefore, strengthened. Those that are used less will fade away. A child's interactions with the world determine how these connections (wiring) are formed, providing either a strong or weak foundation for all future health and learning."

The Importance of Hands-On Experiences

As children are entering a digital world, it is perhaps more important than ever for children to engage with materials that they can touch, feel, manipulate, and even destroy. Long before a child can develop an understanding of what is shown on the screen of a digital device, she needs to know what that image is in a more tangible way. Touching a screen that shows a kitten and connecting it to something else that is soft and fluffy doesn't provide the sensory-motor information needed to develop real understanding. Knowing that a kitten is fluffy comes from touching it. Knowing that sand will pour in different ways comes from scooping, filling, and dumping. Knowing what is at the firehouse comes from planning the trip before you go, making predictions of what will be there, actually visiting, and then comparing what we saw with what we thought we would see.

> This is not a cookbook with recipes that must be followed to the letter. It is intended to inspire you and to encourage innovative education.

The activities in this book are based on using real objects and experiences that children can explore over and over again. Real-world experiences are essential for children in the real world ahead. That doesn't happen on a workbook page.

Use drawing, charting, and graphing to document children's concrete experiences.

Included in this book are suggestions for helping children bridge a concrete experience to an abstract representation, often called *recording*. Just like scientists, children can record their wonderment, experiments, and findings to visually show their thinking. This is important because children need to see their thinking written down. When you do this, it shows children that you respect their ideas. It shows them their ideas can be represented in words and images. This is a bridge to reading and writing that validates them as not only thinkers but also as writers!

There are many different ways to help children translate what they have learned about a concept into abstract and artistic representations. This is an important skill because it allows children to apply what they have learned and to demonstrate their understanding, as well as invites them to move to higher levels of thinking. During what Jean Piaget defined as the preoperational stage (usually from two to six years old), children are on a search for representation, and their major task is to master symbolic and representational function.

Throughout the activities in this book, you will see suggestions for children to record their findings. Here are some suggestions for artistic and abstract representation:

- Make field drawings. When children observe during your activity time or outside, invite them to record their observations with drawings. It really doesn't matter if their drawings look anything like what they see. Have drawing paper in your science area. Always take sketchpads outside for playtime. You never know when an amazing discovery will occur.

- Create prediction/results charts. Before testing a concept such as light and shadow, ask children to make predictions about what they think will happen. What will happen when I shine the flashlight on the sheet? What will light shine through? Record these predictions on chart paper with words and drawings. Add the results at the end of the activity, and discuss the findings.

- Generate graphs. Make simple graphs with actual objects or pictorial representations. These are essential for demonstrating information in an abstract format. For example, you can have children take items they are sorting and line them up in a bar graph.

- Take digital field photos. Children can be amazingly adept at using cameras if they are shown correct handling and use. Use digital cameras for children to record their observations and experimentation.

- Record audio field notes. Of course, recordings don't all have to be made on paper. Show children how to use a simple handheld tape recorder, a digital tablet, or your smartphone to record their observations on a walk or in the classroom.

- Develop measurement charts. Observation often involves measuring. When children measure the growth of a mung-seed sprout or the rising of bread dough, use graph paper, strings, ice-cream sticks, or adding-machine tape to record their measurements. Paste these in a row across a recording chart. Children will be able to "read" their findings by reading the images!

The Necessity of Making Mistakes— Developing a Growth Mindset

We all make mistakes, and we all learn from them. But sometimes young children are afraid to try something new because they are concerned that they might not do it right. I was shocked when I realized that children I was teaching, who were as young as three, could be afraid to offer an idea in the group or test an idea. Perhaps it was because they had asked many questions that had a right and wrong answer before they came to school. Questions such as "What color is this?" or "What does the cow say?" have a good chance of the answer being wrong. Often children stop trying.

> *A person who never made a mistake never tried anything new.*
>
> —Albert Einstein (attributed)

But we know that it is so very important for children to freely offer an idea, a way to solve a problem, or a new thought without fear of doing it wrong. One great thing to share with children is that sometimes you make mistakes, and then show how you learn from them. If you are relaxed about mistakes, they can learn to be, too. Children love to help you when you make a mistake. In my keynote speeches, I ask teachers and parents if they have ever played dumb with the children. Many raise their hands, smiling, while others are appalled! When you ask children to help you with a mistake, you send the message that you value their help and thinking.

When free brainstorming, you can let them know that you really don't know the answer but you would love to brainstorm along with them. This levels the playing field and allows for the fun of thinking together. Many of the circle-time suggestions in these themes invite children to brainstorm ideas. It is important from the outset that children realize that you are not looking for one right answer but for many answers.

The work of Stanford psychologist Carol Dweck on what she calls the growth mindset is a helpful perspective on making mistakes and learning. Her studies support the understanding that intelligence is not fixed but is actually dynamic and can be developed through acts of learning. Her book *Mindset: The New Psychology of Success* encourages people to take risks of thinking, to engage in challenges, and to learn from mistakes. It is all food for the brain. She feels that children's success in handling future situations lies in being willing to

> *Vision is the art of seeing what is invisible to others.*
>
> —Jonathan Swift, Irish author and satirist

recognize the potential to grow through challenges and mistakes. She says, "Some students start thinking of their intelligence as something fixed, as carved in stone. They worry about, 'Do I have enough? Don't I have enough?' Other children think intelligence is something you can develop your whole life. You can learn. You can stretch. You can keep mastering new things." She feels that children with a growth mindset, who think their intelligence will grow through life, are the children who will succeed in school and in life. We can support this by helping children feel great about the journey of learning with all the bumps and falls along the way. And maybe those mistakes will become a great invention, a new way to do something, or a beautiful piece of art.

The Art and Wisdom of Problem Solving

Creativity is allowing yourself to make mistakes. Art is knowing which ones to keep.

—Scott Adams, cartoonist, author of *Dilbert*

In the early childhood years, children are developing the social and emotional ability to handle challenges, use self-control, and persevere. One key skill in discovering the art and wisdom of problem solving is the ability to tolerate frustration and challenges. You can watch children through the year and see how they progress from giving up or smashing things when frustrated to sticking with something until they figure it out. Problem-solving activities help children learn how to identify a problem, think about solutions, and try them out. Interestingly, children who are willing to work out a problem develop a better attention span and ultimately a stronger sense of self. These combined skills provide a sense of security that allows them to try and take appropriate risks. As children develop the ability to think abstractly, they can think about a problem or situation without having to be in the middle of it. This is when our "What would happen if" questions really work and help children consider many options and consequences.

Perhaps best of all, as children learn problem-solving skills they begin to have an increased awareness of not only their own problems but also other people's problems. They can grasp larger issues that affect the planet and people everywhere. At this stage, children can discuss issues such as pollution, endangered animals, and drought. Use children's books and magazines to introduce the topics. Don't shy away from these big issues. Young children have an opinion, and it is often fascinating!

Skills for Exploring Learning Themes

Whatever you do may seem insignificant to you, but it is most important that you do it.

—Mohandas K. Gandhi, leader of the Indian independence movement

Years ago, I called my approach to educational themes the "drop in the bucket" theory. My thinking is that children's understanding expands like the ripples caused by dropping a stone in a bucket full of water. The ever-expanding circles of understanding always start with the self and radiate from the most familiar (home and family) to the less and less familiar (neighborhood and the world beyond). Here is a list of some of the skills children use as their understanding spreads out from self to the world and how these skills apply to the themes of this book.

- How I See the World: Observing and Comparing

    Young children are:

    - examining and comparing the world around them;
    - beginning to explore the world with five senses;
    - noticing similarities and differences between themselves and others;
    - developing a self-image and a social identity;

- discerning physical differences between themselves and others;

- exploring personal uniqueness within a group;

- building self-awareness and confidence in a group;

- sharing personal feelings and stories about themselves; and

- using spatial and prepositional concepts in play and language.

● How I Interact With the World: Needs and Feelings

Young children are:

- recognizing their own needs and the needs of others;

- investigating their physical capabilities and challenges with interest;

- learning the importance of personal body care;

- naming family members and their relationships;

- listening to the feelings of family members and friends;

- using blocks and dramatic-play materials to explore the concept of *home*;

- becoming aware of the sequence of family activities in the home;

- enjoying being helpful with daily family tasks and routines;

- participating in creating family rules;

- sharing information about events and changes in the family;

- constructing homes with art materials;

- acting out family roles in the dramatic-play area;

- noticing the different types of animal homes;

- noticing the needs of animals and plants;

- exploring the concept of the need for shelter;

- learning how to care for a classroom animal; and

- developing a sensitivity to the needs of living things.

- How I Live in the World: Play and Work

  Young children are:

  - discussing the roles family members play;

  - sharing stories of family experiences;

  - developing friendships within the classroom;

  - participating in creating classroom rules;

  - monitoring fair implementation of rules;

  - building social problem-solving skills;

  - learning how to share with others;

  - exploring the work and tools of people in the community;

  - noticing and reading signs in the neighborhood;

  - discussing the work that family and community members do;

  - matching appropriate tools to work and place;

  - comparing the diversity of people in school and neighborhood; and

  - developing an understanding of safe and unsafe activities.

- How I Experience the World: Change

  Young children are:

  - observing growth and change in themselves and others;

  - observing the animals and plants in the world around them;

  - comparing the similarities and difference in animals and plants;

  - recognizing the different habits of animals;

  - examining the many ways animals grow and change;

  - comparing their own personal characteristics (weight, size, hair, and so on) with those of animals;

  - creating observation recordings of experiments and field explorations;

  - exploring science and math tools in classroom experiments;

  - choosing and testing tools to solve a given problem;

  - understanding the importance of safety when handling tools;

  - observing the changes around them (weather, seasons, people, plants);

  - recording observations in charts, graphs, and drawings;

  - predicting changes, such as weather or growth, based on observations;

  - marking passage of time with images and recognizable sequences;

  - developing understanding of the concepts of *yesterday, today,* and *tomorrow*; and

  - exploring the concepts of *long ago* and *now*.

Communicating with Families

Families often ask teachers what they can do at home to support what is happening in school. They want to feel like they are helping to prepare their child for the wide world ahead. Often they think helping means that they need to buy workbooks for skill reinforcement! It is our job to help parents see that the best way they can prepare their children is to help them understand how reading, writing, math, and science are a part of their lives. These skills are not just something to do at school but are integral to living and learning.

You can share these simple and practical tips for parents over the course of many weeks. These tips are purposefully focused on reading books with children. This is because families may not want to do a science or art project at home with their child, but they are likely to read a book. Choose a few at a time to share and send home. If you like, you can expand on the tips that relate the books to something you are doing in school. Invite families to share what they are doing, too. We are all learning together!

What Families Can Do to Support Their Children's Learning

Read books. Read books. Read books! One of the best ways to support a child's learning is to provide a wide variety of books. Young children like books about real things such as people, school, science, nature, and tools. But they also like make-believe, monsters, jokes, and silly rhymes.

I touch the future. I teach.
—Christa McAuliffe, American teacher and astronaut

Read picture books that represent a wide variety of cultures and habitats. This helps the child develop a sense of her place in the world. The following are some tips to use with children:

- Take trips to the library with a specific purpose in mind, such as looking for books that relate to a child's interest or classroom theme.
- Look for books that focus on family relationships with work and play.
- Choose books that not only share a story but also teach concepts such as weather, past and future, water, homes and shelter, and animals.
- Invite a child to compare herself with the characters in a book by asking questions such as, "How are you and the character alike? How are you different? How would you have handled the situation in the story?"
- Ask a child what she notices about a character's needs, feelings, and actions.
- Invite a child to talk about the story sequence: What happens first, in the middle, and at the end?
- Ask a child to retell a story in her own words.
- Encourage a child to predict what a story is about based on the cover illustration.
- Use books to start a conversation together. Talk about the story you read together, and ask what a child thinks about the story.

- Create reading rituals at specific times of the day. A book before school or upon arriving home can be a special personal time with a parent that reinforces what is happening at school.

- Provide a special place for the child's own library. It can be as simple as a basket from the dollar store placed in her room.

- Check with the teacher for the monthly theme. Choose books around the theme, and place them in the child's library

- Go to the public or school library every other week.

- Celebrate how a child memorizes a story—an essential first step to reading!

- Ask the child to read books to a family member, but do not expect the reading to be word-for-word.

- Encourage the child to play with humor, jokes, stories, and rhymes. Humor builds synaptic connections in the brain.

- Make silly mistakes such as holding the book upside-down or starting to read from the back of the book. Correcting an adult is empowering for a child and builds self-esteem.

- Make mistakes by saying the wrong word or pointing to the wrong illustration. The child will enjoy correcting you!

- Ask open-ended questions such as, "What would happen if . . . ?"

- Write, write, write!

- Invite a child to draw pictures inspired by a book or topic.

- Provide paper and markers for the child to draw and "write" her own stories.

- Write down the words the child dictates about her drawings.

- Keep file cards and markers available for taking a child's dictation about everything from drawings to discussions.

- Show a child how to write her name on things, but don't expect the child's writing to be perfect. Make this fun, not a task!

- Create homemade books together. For example, use a digital camera to take photos of a family event to use in a book.

- Use photos to sequence a family event or the growth of a baby brother or sister.

- Demonstrate and share all forms of writing, such as list making, message taking, and thank-you cards.

- Set up a writing area in the house, with paper, magazines, pens, and crayons, where the child can go to draw or write spontaneously.

Remember, open-ended discussions and explorations help all children become contributing members of the world community. When we respect the thoughts, feelings, and the voices of children, we celebrate their culture, their place in the world, and them!

How I See the World— The Art of Observing and Comparing

To acquire knowledge one must study, but to acquire wisdom one must observe.

—Marilyn vos Savant, American writer

Perceiving is the first step in understanding the world around us. We use our skills of observing and comparing to perceive the similarities and differences in our world at home and beyond. Children are excellent at observing and comparing. They often will notice and ask about the smallest detail of a difference. Their curiosity and guileless questions help them make sense of what is an ever-expanding world around them. By focusing on perception and perspective, the activities in this chapter help children take their natural curiosity and apply it to their everyday life at school and home. The activities invite children to look and look again, listen and listen again. Within each activity are multiple opportunities for children to observe and compare a topic from many viewpoints and with a variety of processes. This will help children prepare to be a part of the global world of learning. With an unpredictable future of change ahead for our children, an understanding of same and different is vital.

This section looks at traditional themes with new eyes and a broader perspective, both personal and global at the same time. Let's take a new look at these topics:

- Letters, names, and initials
- Lines and writing
- Sounds
- Opposites
- Faces
- Bodies
- Muscles and movement
- The sense of seeing
- Seeing with all my senses

Playing with Names

There is probably nothing more personal to a young child than her name. It is a way children define and identify themselves, and children can learn a great deal about each other by exploring names. Children will begin to compare the look and sounds of each other's names. Names are also a wonderful way to experience the diversity of the world around us. As children learn to see and say the names of their classroom friends, they are also learning about the sounds of the world community.

Learning Skills

Observing and comparing

Listening and speaking

Name recognition

Function of print

Self-esteem

Materials

Chart paper or whiteboard

5" x 8" file cards or oak tag

Photos of children (optional)

Clear plastic shoe bag or adhesive pockets

Plain white stickers

White drawing paper

Markers, crayons

Collage materials, such as yarn, scrap paper, sequins, craft feathers, and so on

Oak tag or other heavy paper

Glue and glue sticks

Clear self-adhesive paper

Ahead of Time

- Create an attendance board for the children's names. Use a clear plastic shoe bag with pockets, or make your own board with stick-on pockets available at an office supply store.

- Create a name card for each child with or without the child's photo on it. Don't forget to make one for yourself, too!

Let's Get Inspired

- Your circle time is the best place to begin a discussion on names. With attendance, job charts, and name songs, you can celebrate everyone's name. Begin by talking about your own name. You can choose to use your first, last, or both names. You might want to share a bit about how you got your name and why it is special to you. Show a card with your name on it. This will allow children to make the connection between the name you say and how it is written. "This is my name! Can you read it with me? Ellen. *E-L-L-E-N*. Ellen. My grandmother's name was Ellen, too! Let's look at your names."

- Pull out a name card from your collection, and see if anyone can recognize the name or the photo. Ask, "Do you know this name? Yes! Sharma. This is what Sharma's name looks like. *S-H-A-R-M-A*. Sharma." Invite the child to share something about the name. Give the card to the child and go on to the next card.

- Once all children have their name cards, you can play a circle name game sung to the tune of "Way Down Yonder in the Pawpaw Patch." Place all the name cards in the center of the circle and shuffle them. Have the children stand in a circle around the names as they move around singing.

  Where, oh where is our friend Sharma?
  Where, oh where is our friend Sharma?
  Where, oh where is our friend Sharma?
  Here she is in the pawpaw patch!

- At another circle time, introduce the attendance board. Ask the children to find their matching name pocket on the board. Explain that they are to place their name cards in the pockets as a way of showing they are at school. As a part of your daily ritual, show each name one at a time and ask children to identify it and place it in the correct pocket. This will introduce children to the function of print as well as letter and sound recognition.

- Over time, you might want to continue your circle-time exploration into names by inviting family members to visit the circle and share about their names. This is a great way to share the diverse culture of names within the classroom family.

Let's Go!

What is in a name? To a child—everything! In your activity centers, provide children with a wide variety of activities that celebrate and focus on the beauty that is their name. With these activities your children will think, "My name is everywhere!"

- Make personalized placemats and name cards for snack or lunchtime. Not only will children learn to recognize their names, but they will quickly learn others' names as well. Provide heavy white drawing paper, markers, and crayons for making placemats. Children can freely draw on both sides of the paper to create a one-of-a-kind placemat of their own design. Use white stick-on labels to create nametags to place on each side of the placemat. Children will quickly learn each other's names as they try to make sure their friends are sitting next to them for a meal! (These will last all year if you laminate them or cover them with self-adhesive clear vinyl.)

- Place cards are a nice variation and addition to this activity. Give children 5" x 8" cards folded in half lengthwise to create their own place cards. Encourage them to decorate the cards and write their names in precise print. When it is time to eat, children can match their place cards to their placemats. This encourages visual discrimination and name recognition for a purpose!

- During an activity time, invite children to explore the name cards from the attendance board. Bring the cards to a table, and ask children to notice the similarities and differences. "Can you find names that are the same length?" "Can you find names that start with similar letters?" "Can you find names that end with similar letters?" Children can sort the names in groups of differing attributes.

- Create a name treasure hunt around the room. Write children's names on simple stick-on labels, and hide the names around the room. Don't press the label on too tightly so that children can easily take it off when they find it. Give children a piece of paper to collect their name treasures as they hunt around the room. "How many did you find?"

- Write a class name book together! Each child gets a two-page spread to draw a picture of herself on one side and write her name on the other. Children will enjoy turning the pages of this class book and seeing their friends represented there. This can be laminated, or place the pages in a magnetic (adhesive) photo album for durability.

Expanding the Understanding

- Take the name play outside on a beautiful day for some name team cheering! Have children sit in two lines across from each other. Use a cheer to spell out children's names and cheer for them. When children hear their names fully spelled, they can run to the other side and sit down. You can use the name cards to help children visualize the letters.

Give me a C!
Give me an a!
Give me an r!
Give me an l!
Give me an o!
Give me an s!
What does it spell?
Carlos!
Hooray for Carlos! He's our friend!

- Introduce a new stuffed animal or doll to the classroom. Invite children to suggest a name for it. Make a chart of the names, and ask them to vote for their favorite.
- Involve the families. Send children home with a small booklet for the family to add their names and any drawings or photos if they like. Children can explore the concept that Dad or Mom has a first name, too!

Playing with the Letters of My Name

The letters children learn first are the ones in their own names. They are also interested in the names of their friends, so these letters become fascinating, too. When you create a focus on the children's names throughout your classroom environment, you will be building essential observation and visual-discrimination skills as well as self-awareness. Children will begin to recognize the letters of their names and the names of their friends. This skill quickly translates to the larger world around them as children begin to recognize the letters that appear in their names in the signs they see in their community.

Learning Skills

Visual Discrimination

Matching

Observing and Comparing

Self-Awareness

Materials

Alphabet letter strip or alphabet cards

Easel paper

Oak tag (or 5" x 8" file cards)

Markers, crayons, and/or easel paint

Envelopes

Scissors

Play clay or playdough

Photos of each child (optional)

Wide-square graph paper

Ahead of Time

- Create individual letter cards for each child's first initial. Use oak tag or other stiff paper to create a card that children can use over and over again. If possible, place a photo of each child on the card and a large first letter of the child's name. Younger children can just have their photo and the initial. Older children can have the large first letter and smaller letters for the rest of the name.

- Cut large letters from oak tag or file cards for making puzzles.

- Hang an alphabet letter strip near your circle time so that the children can refer to it during the activity.

Let's Get Inspired

- Use the initial name cards to get the activity going at circle time. Begin with a game to introduce the cards. Place the cards in the center of the circle, and invite the children to notice and observe the similarities and differences in them. Ask, "What do you see? Do you know any of these letters?" For older children, ask, "Do you know any of these names?" Children will probably be very excited to see their own and others' names depicted with letters on the cards.

- Encourage the excitement by inviting children to take turns finding their own card and letter. Ask, "What letter starts your name? Do you see any other cards that start with the same letter? Let's look and see."

- Children whose names start with the same letter can come and stand next to each other. Ask, for example, "Whose name starts with *A*? Come and join me up front! Wow! We have three children whose names start with *A*: Alison, Ahmal, and Andy. Let's say the names together." Go through all the names.

- Add a song for each letter sung to the tune of "Row, Row, Row Your Boat":
  A, A, A it is.
  A is our first letter.
  Alison, Ahmal, Andy, A! (Note: if there is only one child, just repeat the name)
  They all start with A!

- At another circle time, you can use the alphabet strip placed at eye level so that the children can interact easily with it. Ask the children to find the first letter in their names on the alphabet strip. One at a time, they can show the letter and match the card. Ask, "How many people have names that start with *R*? Let's count and see."

Let's Go!

- Throughout the week, children can use their initial letter cards to work with the letters in their names. Provide children with easel paper and paint or markers to use to draw or paint their initials. Encourage them to use large strokes to make large letters. Ask, "Can you fill your page with your initial? How many ways can you make the letter *N*? (Note: it is important to start big with letters, and free exploration of the shape of the initial is a great way to do it!)

- Invite children to go on an initial hunt around the room. Ask them to take their cards with them and to look for words in the environment that have that letter in it. It doesn't have to be the first letter in the word. The purpose is to recognize the letter in the environment.

- Another day, take children for a walk around the building to find more letters that match.

- Children can learn more about their first letter by creating personal initial letter puzzles. Provide each child with a large initial letter to decorate with crayons and markers. Help the children cut their letters into three large pieces to create a jigsaw puzzle. Provide an envelope to store the puzzles for children to decorate with their letter or name. Keep the initial puzzles in the literacy area for frequent use.

- Provide play clay or playdough, and encourage the children to create their initial letters. Sculpting the shape of the letter helps children feel the form of the letter and provides essential tactile feedback to hands.

Expanding the Understanding

- Graph your initial! Make a simple vertical alphabet chart on wide-square graph paper. Children can use crayons to color in the square next to their initial letter. When the graph is complete, ask, "Which letter do most children share as an initial? Which letter do we have the least? Are there any letters with no initials? Why?"

- Do an initial dance! Use the song and game of "The Farmer in the Dell." Children can hold their initial letter cards as they dance around the circle. When the farmer calls their letter, they can move into the center of the circle.

The farmer takes an A!
The farmer takes an A!
High-ho my initial!
The farmer takes an A!

- At snack time, provide plain crackers and "squeeze cheese" for children to take turns drawing their initials on their snack. This can also work with plain cookies and frosting tubes!

Playing with Lines

Lines are a major component of letter writing. Vertical, horizontal, and diagonal lines are essential to writing many of the letters in our alphabet. Let's explore the nature of lines through noticing their similarities and differences. Children will begin to build an understanding of lines and the many ways to make them. The ability to communicate ideas is the basis of collaborating with those who share the world with us.

Learning Skills

Writing

Drawing

Eye-hand coordination

Observing and comparing

Materials

Chart paper or whiteboard

Markers, crayons, and large pencils

Yarn

Drawing and fingerpaint paper

Fingerpaints

Chalk

White glue

Index cards

Tempera paint and brushes

Ahead of Time

Prepare a variety of papers with one interesting straight or curved line on each. Be sure they are all different.

Let's Get Inspired

- Start your exploration of lines at circle time, and expand it into all areas of the classroom. Begin with a game. As you gather the children for circle, draw their attention to your chart paper or whiteboard. Draw a simple line across the paper horizontally. Ask, "What did I do? What did I make?" Children may or may not say, "A line." Accept all answers equally, and if it is not offered say, "I made a line."

- Invite the children to look around the circle and the room for other examples of lines. There might be small lines in a striped shirt or big ones along the ceiling tiles. The object of this is to invite the children to notice the different lines that are around them.

- Ask, "How are the lines the same?" Take time to hear their answers before you ask them, "How are they different?" Be sure to separate these two questions. This searching game could go on for days. Just get the idea started, and be ready to play this again and again.

- Now add another line to the original line you drew. For example, you can draw a line perpendicular to the first line to begin creating a rectangle. Keep asking children what they see in your lines as you continue to draw. "What does this look like to you?" "What line should I add next?"

- Eventually complete the rectangle, and invite the children to use creative thinking to imagine what the shape might be. "What do these lines make you think of?" It could be a birdhouse, or a TV, or a stove. Write children's ideas on chart paper.

- Tell the children that they are going to be Line Explorers, discovering all kinds of lines.

Let's Go!

- After circle time, invite a small group of children to join you in the art area. Remind them of the discussion about lines, and then show them the prepared papers with different lines on them. Hold up the papers, and invite the children to suggest what each line reminds them of. Ask, "What could the line become if you added more lines to it?"

- Invite the children to choose a paper and use crayons and markers to continue adding lines to create an image. Reassure them that there is no right or wrong way to do this. Encourage them to be creative and "think outside the line!"

- Encourage the children to tell something about their drawings when they are done. Write their words on index cards that can be displayed with their line images on a bulletin board.

- Expand the learning by exploring the lines with a variety of different media:
    - Over a period of time, set out fingerpaints and paper for line making.
    - Provide clay or playdough for sculpting lines and using them to create images.
    - Provide large sheets of mural paper, tempera paint, and brushes for making giant line images.
    - White glue in squeeze bottles can be used to create lines for gluing lengths of yarn.

- Eventually lead the line making to letter making. Continue the focus on lines and letters in the literacy center with a variety of activities that will reinforce the concept. Gather the children together, and demonstrate how lines can make some letters. Draw a vertical line, and then add a horizontal line in the middle. Ask, "Does this look like a letter you know? What line should I add to create the letter?"

- Go through the alphabet looking for straight lines.

- Ask, "Do you have any straight lines in your name? How many?"

- Create a list of letters with straight lines to post on the wall.

Expanding the Understanding

- Take your lines outside. Provide children with chalk to make all kinds of lines on the sidewalk and pavement of the playground. They can become sidewalk artists as they draw lines.

- Later in the week, expand the activity by drawing dots on the pavement and asking children to draw lines between them. Ask, "What did we create together?"

- Experiment with lines by playing a variety of line-up games throughout the study. For example, over time you can have children line up by different physical qualities, such as boy, girl, boy, girl; hair color; type of shoes; or clothing. Practice physically making lines with a line-up game. Call children to line up according to the colors they are wearing. Start with red and move to orange, yellow, and so on. In the end you just might have a rainbow line!

- Try singing a line-up song to the tune of "London Bridge Is Falling Down":

    Listen, children. Listen, children.
    Line up now. Make a line.
    Listen, children. Make a line.
    Everybody line up.

- Do a line dance such as Peanut Butter and Jelly or Who Stole the Cookies from the Cookie Jar.

- Invite parents to participate. Ask them to go on a line hunt with their child at home and look for many examples of lines.

- Encourage children to explore the names of all family members to see how many letters with straight lines are in each name. Collect the information for the child to share in school.

Playing with Sounds

Children will experiment with both making and hearing sounds and will begin to discriminate the differences among them. The world is filled with sound. Some sounds are familiar, and others are new and interesting. The ability to listen to and repeat sounds helps children appreciate the diversity of the many beautiful sounds in the world.

Learning Skills

Auditory discrimination

Listening

Observing and comparing sounds

Vocalizing and sound matching

Materials

Prerecorded environmental sounds on a cell phone, tablet, or computer

Small objects that make different sounds when dropped

Bag or pillowcase

Small cardboard boxes

Paper towel tubes

Painter's or masking tape

Sand, pebbles, bells, coins, and other small objects to make a variety of sounds

Recording device

CDs of a variety of musical styles

Markers, pens, and crayons

Mural paper

Yard stick

Ahead of Time

- Prepare a recording of environmental sounds from around your home, outside, in the park, in the store, and so on. You can use the recording function on your cell phone, tablet, or computer. Some websites have recorded sounds you can use.

- Collect a variety of small objects that will make a sound when dropped, such as a bell, a book, a ball, a rattle, and so on. Hide these in a bag or pillowcase.

Let's Get Inspired

Sounds are all around us, but sometimes we need to pay attention to them to understand their sources and purposes. Here are a few activities for your circle time to get the concept of listening and making sounds going.

- Start with a fun listening game. Play a series of simple prerecorded sounds for the children to identify. You might want to play a sound and ask, "What do you hear? What made that sound? Was it an animal, a person, or an object?" If you want to expand the conversation, you can also ask, "Where do you think this happened? Is it in the city or the country? How do you know?"

- Sounds have a purpose. Listen to the sounds, and talk about how the sound might help us. For example, the sound of an ambulance tells a driver to get out of the way. The sound of a doorbell tells us someone is at the door. What does the sound of a baby crying tell us? What does the sound of a dog barking suggest?

- Stop for a moment and ask the children to just listen to the sounds in and around the room. What do the sounds tell us? Perhaps we hear a lawnmower out front or a train going by. Or maybe we hear the sound of the air conditioner. These are all sound messages that tell us what is happening in our environment.

- Sing a sound song to the tune of "Did You Ever See a Lassie?" After several verses, invite the children to suggest the new sound for the song.

> *Did you ever hear a drum beat, a drum beat, a drum beat?*
> *Did you ever hear a drum beat go tappity tap?*
> *Did you ever hear a cat sound, a cat sound, a cat sound?*
> *Did you ever hear a cat sound go meow, meow, meow, meow?*
> *Did you ever hear a door close, a door close, a door close?*
> *Did you ever hear a door close: slam, bam, bam, bam!*

Let's Go!

A sense of hearing helps us navigate the world around us. In the following activities, children can observe and compare the sounds they hear and the sounds they can make.

- Play What Fell? Tell the children to put on their listening ears. Demonstrate how something makes a sound when you drop it by dropping a small block in front of the children: Bang! Invite the children to close their eyes and open their ears as you drop something for them to guess. Ask, "What was it? What fell?" You can experiment with adding the sense of sight as well as sound. For example, you can show children the collection of objects before you drop one. This may help children guess what fell. But then try it with surprise objects that they have not seen. After several rounds, give the children a bag and have them go around the room to find something to drop for the others to guess.

- Play Match My Sound! This is a great way to play with auditory discrimination and vocalization. Make a sound, and ask the children to repeat it. Make another sound, and have them replicate it, too. They will catch on very quickly to the give-and-take nature of this game. Vary the sounds: long sounds, short sounds, abrupt sounds, and melodic sounds. Change the rhythm and beats of the sounds, too. You will be building skills needed for learning the sounds of letters and words.

- Record voices. Many children are surprised to hear what they sound like when their voice is recorded. If possible, record the children saying their names, making a favorite sound, and/ or singing a simple song. You can also record a discussion about their favorite TV show or activity to do. Play the recording back for them. Ask, "How do you sound? Did you sound like you?" You can also have each child record the same simple sentence such as, "I go to the Rainbow Preschool," or "It is going to rain today." At circle time, play the recorded sentences back and invite the children to guess whose voice it is!

- Provide the children with recyclable materials to make sound machines. You can use small boxes and tubes to hold small objects that will make a sound if shaken. Seal the containers with tape. Try using sand and other quiet noisemakers as well as loud items such as bells and small stones. Invite the children to listen to the different sounds and sort them in different ways, such as soft versus loud or metal versus paper sounds.

Expanding the Understanding

- We need sounds to make words and conversation! Invite children to make sounds instead of words to communicate with a friend. Can you have a sound conversation?

- A classic and always favorite sound activity for young children is drawing to music. There is something so very simple and yet rewarding about moving a crayon or marker to the different genres of music. Tape a giant piece of mural paper on the floor, and invite children to "belly up" to the paper as they stretch out and draw as the music plays. Choose a wide variety of musical sounds from around the world. The Putumayo collection of recorded world music for children has many wonderful selections.

- Go for a listening walk in the playground or within the school. The challenge is for children to not make noise as they listen for the sounds around them. Come back to class and talk about what you heard and how it felt.

Playing with Opposites

Understanding opposites provides children with an important tool for noticing similarities and differences in the world around them. This ability is not only a key language skill but also is an essential ingredient in making and understanding math and science comparisons. Children will experiment with matching and creating opposites using familiar objects as well as their own bodies.

Learning Skills

Verbal communication skills

Comparative vocabulary

Observing and comparing opposites

Matching

Extrapolating opposites from known to unknown

Materials

Sets of opposite objects, such as large and small blocks, books, crayons, and envelopes

A collection of rocks in different sizes, colors, shapes, and textures

Yarn

Craft paper

Magazines and wrapping paper

Safety scissors

Glue sticks or glue

Pan balance (optional)

Let's Get Inspired

Your circle time is the best place to start children thinking about and experiencing fun opposites. When children use their bodies, they incorporate the concept in their muscle memory as well as their minds. Let's get playing with opposites!

- Begin with a bit of silliness. Find some fun ways to get children thinking of opposites. You can carefully walk backward into circle time. Or hold your book backward, and start reading from the end of the book. You can try greeting everyone with your final circle song instead of your hello song. Or tell them it is time to go home! They will soon catch on that you are saying the opposite of what you mean.

- Try an opposites game to get children involved in the fun. Invite everyone to stand up, and then do the opposite. Ask them to lean back, and then lean forward instead. You can explore moving forward and back or to the right and the left. You can shout and whisper or move near and far. Invite a child to do a move and the others to think of the opposite!

- At another circle time, play an Opposites Simon Says game. This can be tricky, so save it for later in this exploration time. The leader says for everyone to reach up high and then everyone is to do the opposite and reach down low. Nobody is sent out of the game. Just have a good laugh and try it again.

Let's Go!

In your activity times you can explore the process of observing and comparing with math, science, language, and art awareness. Play an opposites matching game. Place your collection of objects in the center of an activity table. Invite children to observe and compare the items. Ask, "How are they alike?" "How are they different?" "Can you find pairs of objects that go together in a particular way?" Children can group the opposites together and discuss the differences that they see.

- Extend the learning by asking children to explore the room and look for pairs of opposites to add to the collection. They might find short and long pencils, empty and full paste containers, big and little books, and so on.

- Introduce Venn diagrams. Use two pieces of yarn tied together to make Venn diagram circles. Make them large so that the items the children are using will fit inside. The children might do a Venn diagram of big and little, dark and light, or rough and smooth. If you want to focus on a specific material, try using stones and rocks. These can be compared in size, shape, color, and texture!

- Make an opposites word wall. Children like to play with new vocabulary, and word walls are a great way to make the words visual. Use poster board or your whiteboard to make a list of words and their opposites. Start with one word, and ask the children to suggest the opposite word. Invite children to draw or cut out pictures to illustrate the words on the wall. Send home a photo of the word wall to parents so that they can see what the children are doing in class.

- Make an opposites collage. Children can use their observational skills by hunting through magazines for examples of opposites. This is not as easy as it sounds. You may have to give them a set of parameters to help with the search. For example, they could search for soft and hard, heavy and light, or empty and full. Put these pictures together in a class *Big Book of Opposites*.

Expanding the Understanding

- One of the best ways to make a concept real for children is to take it out into the world. Gather the children and take an opposites walk in the school and neighborhood. Look for red and green lights, big and little cars, tall and low buildings, open and closed windows and doors, short and tall trees, and so on. What else can they find? If possible, carry a clipboard to write down some of your discoveries. Take the information back to class for a discussion.

- Have an opposites day. Send home a note to families to explain what you have been studying and your plan for the day. When the children arrive, say goodbye! Reverse the order of things in the day. Start with snack or activity time and work toward your morning circle! You could start with outside, too. Just shake things up a bit and do the opposites. At the end of the day in your circle time, ask the children to share their experience of the day.

- Extend the Venn! Bring out your pan-balance scale for children to explore the different rocks in terms of heavy and light.

- The song "The Noble Duke of York" is perfect for opposites. Children use their bodies to explore *up* and *down* with each stanza.

> *Oh, the noble Duke of York,*
> *He had ten thousand men.*
> *He marched them up to the top of the hill,* (stand up)
> *And he marched them down again.* (crouch down)
> *Oh when you're up, you're up.* (stand up)
> *And when you're down, you're down.* (crouch down)
> *And when you are only halfway up,* (stop in a mid-crouch)
> *You're neither up nor down!* (stand up and crouch down)

My Face, Your Face

Perhaps one of the best ways to prepare children for a global world is to help them to see the beauty in the many faces that are part of it. People have the basic same parts: eyes, nose, mouth, and ears, but there are so many wonderful variations. These activities invite children to first explore their own faces and then to look out into the world of faces around them. Children will begin to notice the similarities and differences in the many faces of people.

Learning Skills

Observing and comparing visual differences and similarities

Self-awareness

Social interaction

Empathy

Materials

Poster or whiteboard

Markers

Photos of many different faces

Safety mirrors

Paper and paint

Craft paper and glue sticks

Magazines

Scissors

Collage materials

Lamp or flashlight

Ahead of Time

- Collect photos of a wide variety of faces from magazines or an image search online. These will be used for a variety of activities throughout the exploration.
- Cut out paper eyes in the basic colors of brown, blue, green, and hazel. These will be used in an eye graph.

Let's Get Inspired

You can start the concept in your circle time with a variety of group activities and games. This will help children all get on the same page with the concept you will be exploring over the next few days or week.

- Start the fun by making a funny face! Anything you do will get children's attention, and they will certainly be looking at your face. Invite them to make silly faces, too. You can even experiment with making a face and inviting them to copy it. Then, they can make one for you to copy.

- All of these funny faces will lead into a wonderful opportunity to talk about faces. Invite the children to notice the different parts of your face that you move. You might make a crooked smile or cross your eyes or scrunch your nose. Focus on each facial feature one at a time to emphasize the differences.

- Help the children notice the similarities and differences in all the classroom faces with a simple chant. Repeat the chant several times, inviting them to look around the circle at the different faces.

> *My face,* (point to your face)
> *Your face,* (point to someone else's face)
> *His face, her face,* (point to another person's face)
> *We all have a face.*
> *They are all different,*
> *But each face has two eyes,* (point to eyes)
> *One nose,* (point to nose)
> *One mouth,* (point to mouth)
> *And two ears.* (point to ears)
> *Hooray for faces!* (smile)

Let's Go!

Invite the children to explore the four basic features of eyes, ears, nose, and mouth. This is a great way for them to notice their own faces and then notice similarities and differences in the faces of others.

- Make a face chart. You can start this one day and continue it through the study. Gather a small group of children at an activity table to help you create a face chart. Start at the top of the face by talking about the eyes first. Write the word *eyes* at the top of the chart, and draw two eyes next to it. Invite children to brainstorm all the different ways we use our eyes. You can help them by giving them a sentence starter such as, "Eyes are for . . ." Talk with the children about how we can communicate with our eyes without even using words. Ask, "What can your eyes 'say'?" Challenge them to use just their eyes to express anger, fear, happiness, or sleepiness. Write the children's ideas on the chart.

- Make an eye graph. Encourage children to notice each other's eyes. Ask, "Do we all have the same color eyes?" "How are eyes the same?" "How are they different?" Use the cut-out eyes on a sheet of paper to make a simple bar graph of eye colors. The children can add their eye color to the correct bar in the graph. Ask, "Which color do we have the most of?"

- Continue the face chart: Explore ears, noses, and mouths throughout the week. Each day focus on one particular facial feature, and ask the children, "What do you use ears (a nose, a mouth) for?" At the end you will have a great collection of their thoughts written on a chart. Celebrate all the many different faces in the class.

- Create "my face–your face" portraits. This is a great activity to do at the easel but it can also be done at an art table. Invite the children to paint their own portraits. If possible, provide large safety mirrors for children to use to study their own features as they paint. Then invite the children to paint a portrait of a friend! Show the children how to sit for their portraits as their artist friend paints them. Display the portraits on a My Face–Your Face bulletin board. You can add photos of children to the display, too.

● Explore facial symmetry. Use your collected photos of many different faces for children to explore the similarities and differences in the faces in the world. Help children see the similarities by pointing out how faces are usually symmetrical. You can show this by using a piece of paper to show only half of a face. Then move the paper to the other side to show the other half. Take the paper away to see how the face is similar on both sides and now whole. Give children paper to try this out on the different faces. At the end of the activity, encourage children to make a collage of the many faces they have examined.

Expanding the Understanding

● Talk about the many differences the children see in the faces they have studied. We all look different, but we all have the same four main features. But, some faces look so different to us that they might seem strange or even frightening. Encourage children to share their feelings about meeting a new or different face. Can we always remember that these faces may be different from ours but are similar in the same parts?

● Children may also enjoy studying the symmetry in animal faces. Provide books and photos for children to explore in a similar way by covering half an animal's face to see the symmetry on both sides.

● You can use magazine photos of animal faces to make animal face puzzles. Children can paste each face on paper and then cut it in half down the center to make a two-part puzzle. Mix up the pieces and make a collection of puzzles. What happens when you combine a lion face and a bear face?

● Make silhouette face collages. Use a light source such as a strong lamp or flashlight to project light on a white sheet of drawing paper. Have a child sit in the light to make a silhouette of his face. Carefully trace the face, and give the image to the child to cut out. Encourage each child to add collage items, magazine pictures, or anything they want to make a statement: This is me!

My Body, Your Body

In the early years, children are becoming more and more aware of their own bodies and the bodies of others. Sometimes they notice how people are different more than they notice how they are the same. This provides a wonderful opportunity to celebrate how we are the same in some ways but are different in many others. We each have a wonderful body to celebrate, and we can honor the diversity of the world by accepting everyone!

Learning Skills

Observing and comparing physical differences and similarities

Self-awareness

Body awareness

Social interaction

Empathy

Materials

Chart and craft paper

Markers, crayons

Safety scissors

Glue sticks

Three very large shapes, 3 feet wide (circle, square, triangle)

Tape

Measuring tape

Yarn or ribbon

Tempera paint

Large sponges

Stamp pads (optional)

Photo of each child

Ahead of Time

Send home a letter to the families inviting them to share a photo of their family with the class. Each child can bring in a photo to show and share. If families do not have a photo to share, try taking photos of family members and children when they come to pick up their child. Don't forget to bring a childhood family photo of your own, too! If families have their child's birth footprint, ask them if you could borrow that, too.

Let's Get Inspired

Our individual characteristics are different from those of others, but we all have the same basic parts. This study explores the body in much the same way we explored faces. We will notice how we all have hair, arms, legs, and feet. Many of these characteristics are different. This makes us who we are! It is important to encourage children to be positive in their observations of difference. Remember, this is a celebration.

- Celebrate our uniqueness! Start by showing a photo of your family when you were a child or a photo of your current family. Children will be fascinated to see the photos of your family. Encourage them to notice the similarities and differences among the family members. Then invite the children to take turns showing the photos of their families. Encourage the children to name the people in the photo. Does everybody look the same? How are they different? Children may notice first that the adults are bigger than the children. They may notice differences in hair and eye color. Celebrate all the similarities and differences. Children will want to look at the photos after circle time, so place them on a bulletin board or in a small photo album for them to freely examine. (Note: If you're worried about photos getting damaged, just make copies of them for the children to look at.)

- Play a movement game to celebrate the differences in your group. This works well if you have a large circle area, or you may want to take this outside or to the gym. It is a great way to explore sorting and classifying with bodies! Tape three large shapes—a circle, a square, and a triangle—on the floor. You will call out a category and tell the children which shape to walk, hop, or skip to. Start with clothing. For example, say, "Everyone wearing red, walk to the circle." "Everyone wearing blue, hop to the square." "Everyone wearing white, skip to the triangle." Have children count how many are in their shape. Which group has the most? Now change the characteristics to details such as eye color or hair color, long hair or short hair, and so on. Celebrate each group by counting how many and looking to see who shares each group. When a child notices that she shares a quality with others, it gives her a sense of belonging.

- Choose a body part, such as hands, and invite the children to take turns demonstrating something they can do with it. Write down their suggestions on an experience chart and add their names. If possible, take a photo of the child doing her demonstration, and add that to the chart, too. How many different ways can we use our hands? Over time explore other body parts in the same way. How many ways can you use your feet, legs, arms, or head? The possibilities are endless!

Let's Go!
Take the learning into your activity centers and provide the children with many different opportunities to explore their own bodies and to see the similarities and differences in others.

- There is probably nothing more personal than the prints of our hands, feet, and fingers. Often children will have a footprint photo from when they were born. If possible, invite children to share these with the class. How is the baby footprint different from the child's feet now? Invite the children to make footprints. Use a large sponge as a paint pad. Add liquid tempera to the pad and allow it to sink in so it is not slippery. Show the children how to press one foot very lightly onto the surface of the sponge and then press it on a

sheet of paper. Encourage the children to explore their feet in different positions. Ask, "How does your foot look when you are standing on your toes?" How does it look when you are crouching down?" "How about when you are standing tall?" Try it and see the differences.

● How far around is your head? Heads come in many sizes. Give each child a length of yarn or ribbon to act as a nonstandard measuring device. Show them how to wrap it around the widest part of the head like a headband. Cut the length for the child, and hold it up for him to see how big around his head is! Invite the children to go around the room with their "headband" looking for other things that are the same size as their head! Then have children attach their band to a chart to show the different sizes of the heads in the group. Don't forget to measure your head, too! Ask the principal, a cafeteria worker, a parent, and other important people to get measured, too. We all have different-sized heads!

● No two fingerprints are alike. Children are often surprised to find out how different their fingerprints are from those of others. You can extend the foot- and handprint making into a study of finger- and thumbprints. There are actually four different classifications of prints that you can find on a simple Google image search: *whorl, loop, arch,* and *composite*. Children may like to study their own fingerprints using a stamp pad and the images of the four types of prints. Provide magnifiers to explore the fingers, thumbs, and prints up close. Ask questions to invite investigation. "Are your fingerprints the same for each finger?" "Is your thumbprint the same on both hands?" "How is your thumbprint different from a friend's?" Make a chart showing all the fingerprints in the class.

● Using a measuring tape, measure each child's height and record this on chart paper. Occasionally revisit this activity, noticing and commenting on how the children are growing over time.

Expanding the Understanding

● Use the tune of "Mary Wore a Red Dress" to explore similarities and differences in our bodies. Change the words to fit the game.

> *Whoever has brown hair, brown hair, brown hair,*
> *Whoever has brown hair, stand up now.*
> *Twirl around, twirl around, touch the ground.*
> *Whoever has brown hair, smile right now.*

● Each time you sing a verse, have the children who are standing add a movement. They can spin around or jump up and down. Help children notice how even though their hair is all the same color, the styles are different. Some styles are long, and some are short. Some are curly, and some are straight. Hooray for differences!

- You can use plain talcum powder to make prints on the sidewalk. Place the powder in a low plate or pan. Children can gently place one foot in the talc and then have fun running around the sidewalk making prints! Try hands, too. If they are allowed to make handprints on the building, encourage them to do so. Then change the method for another exploration. Have children make foot- and handprints by dipping one foot or hand in water. What do the prints look like now?

- Create a "What My Body Can Do" graph, listing actions from finger snapping to hopping on one foot on the chart. Invite the children to predict how many times they can hop or snap, and then test their predictions! Use tally marks to record the number of times they can hop, skip, or jump.

How My Body Works

Young children are at a wonderful time of discovery as they learn about all the unique parts, functions, and actions of their bodies. It is an important time for children to use their skills of observation and comparison as they develop the fine and large motor skills that will last them a lifetime. This is also an important time to see the universality of bodies and functions in the larger world. In these activities, the children will begin to explore the human body's many parts and their specific functions.

Learning Skills

Observing and comparing

Following directions

Coordination

Counting and tallying

Locomotor movement

Materials

Poster board or whiteboard

Markers

Mural paper

Crayons, large pencils

Safety scissors

Nonbreakable full-length mirror (optional)

Bird and animal photos or cards

Flashlight

Chalk

Rope

Boxes

Hoops

Ahead of Time

If possible, invite family members to bring in a safe animal or bird to class for comparison. Set up different animals on different days so that children can focus their observations.

Let's Get Inspired

- Children are often curious about how their body works. In the early years, they want to learn how to hop and skip, snap their fingers, throw, and catch. How does the body learn how do all that? Explore the body's parts, muscles, and movement together.

- Start with a fun song to get everyone moving! Use the tune of "The Bear Went over the Mountain" with these words:

  > *My fingers are starting to wiggle.* (wiggle fingers)
  > *My fingers are starting to wiggle.*
  > *My fingers are starting to wiggle,*
  > *Around and around and around.*

- Ask, "What other ways can you move your fingers?" They might try to snap or tap, touch, or clap. Add each suggested movement to the song. After singing, discuss all the different ways you moved your fingers.

- Make a "My Fingers Can" chart. After exploring some movements with the song, invite children to brainstorm all the ways they can use their fingers. Write their thoughts on chart paper so that the children feel their ideas are validated by seeing them in print. You might want to draw a big hand with long fingers on the chart and fill in the fingers with their ideas! Ask, "What do you use your fingers for?" "How do they help you when you get up in the morning?" How do they help you when you are eating? playing? working? dressing? speaking?" Leave the chart up so that children can add ideas as they think of them over time.

- Later in the week, do a similar exploration of feet. "How many ways do you use your feet?" "How do they help you do things throughout the day?" Make a similar chart and ask children to compare the different ways they use their hands and feet. Are any of the actions similar?

- Continue the fun by adding familiar body-related songs to your circle time. One of the best is the traditional song "If You're Happy and You Know It," because you can use all the different body parts in the song. Try verses such as "nod your head, cluck your tongue, rub your tummy, lick your lips," and so on. Invite the children to add their own movements and verses.

- You can continue the discussion of body parts and movements throughout the week. What can you do with your head? your tummy? your tongue? Try them all!

- We all use body language to communicate. A nod of the head says something, as does a wink of an eye or the waggle of a finger. Start a discussion of the ways we use our body to "talk" by making a movement and asking the children to guess what you are saying. Be prepared for some giggles!

Let's Go!

During your learning-center time, children can explore their bodies with science, math, and literacy awareness. By expanding to include observation of the bodies of animals, we extend the children's view of the world and help them see how they are more alike than different.

- At this early age, children love to count everything and are especially interested in showing you how many fingers they have. You can start with the body-outline activity using mural paper and crayons. But instead of focusing on the art of the body, tally the parts! Have children stretch out on a piece of mural paper as you carefully draw their outline. Then ask them to count up their different parts, and write the numbers on their drawing. "How many fingers do you have on one hand? on the other?" Help children focus on large and small parts. "How many eyes, ears, feet, tummies, and backs do you have?" At the end of the activity, ask the children to notice what parts of their bodies they have the most of.

- Children can expand their view of bodies by observing and comparing their bodies to those of animals. If possible, real animals are the best for comparisons, but animal photos or cards are also effective. To start, choose a particular type of animal for children to observe and compare. A cat or dog can be a good example, since many children are familiar with them. Make a two-part chart for children to record their findings. One side is for their own bodies, and the other is for the animal's. Record their thoughts as you explore. Ask children to notice characteristics that might be similar and different. "Do you both have hair? How is it the same or different?" "Do you both have hands and feet? How are they the same or different?" "Do you both have noses? How are they different?" "How does the animal use its nose? How do you use yours?" You can continue this exploration over many weeks exploring everything from mammals to birds to fish. This is an excellent opportunity to work with inference as they begin to see the similar and different functions of body parts in all beings.

- My Hands and Feet Can and Can't: This is a fun challenge of thinking and problem solving. Gather a few children around an activity table, and give them simple challenges to solve. For example, you might tell them to pick up a piece of paper with their hands. Then challenge them to pick it up without using their hands! Here are a few others to try:

- ◆ Point to something. Now point without using your hands.

- ◆ Use your feet to make a noise. Now make a noise without your feet.

- ◆ Use your feet to dance. Now dance without using your feet!

● Children will be fascinated to take a look at the bone structure of their hands and feet. All you need is a strong flashlight in a dark room. Children can hold the flashlight up to the body part and examine the muscles and tendons in the hands and feet. Provide art materials for children to draw what they see inside!

Expanding the Understanding

● Hop, skip, and jump. This topic is perfect for outdoor experimenting with large muscle movements. Set up simple hopscotch games on the sidewalk for children to jump and count. Put out boxes and hoops for children to jump in and out of. Older children will enjoy playing with skipping ropes. They may only be able to jump over a stationary rope at first, but they will enjoy the challenge.

● Balancing is an important part of locomotor movements, and children love the challenge. Use chalk and rope as balance beams. Encourage them to experiment with rolling the hoops in a balanced way! How far can you roll a hoop?

● Add all of your favorite movement songs and games to create a Musical Movement Olympics with the children. Use songs such as "Skip to my Lou"; "The Hokey Pokey"; and "Head, Shoulders, Knees, and Toes."

My Sense of Seeing

Young children live in a very intense, multisensory world. Sometimes it is a delight to stand back and look. Invite the children to focus their attention on one sense at a time. As they experiment with observation and explore further, they can add other senses to expand their experience and their understanding. What if children experienced the sense of sight as both a scientist and an artist? What different awareness might arise? Let's visit the sense of sight with "new eyes."

Children will experiment with the sense of sight and other senses and will begin to look at the world around them from different perspectives.

Learning Skills

Observing and comparing

Sorting and classifying

Labeling

Predicting

Sensory motor skills

Deduction

Problem solving

Materials

Variety of interesting objects of different sizes, shapes, and textures, such as pencils, counting cubes, blocks, rocks, sponges, and so on

Something beautiful, such as a peacock feather, a live plant or flower, or a seashell

Drawing paper

Crayons, markers, chalk

Watercolors

Magnifiers

Flashlight

Small brown lunch bags

Cloth or scarf

Measuring tape

Ahead of Time

Prepare a brown paper "surprise" bag for each child. Put one object in each bag, such as a pencil, a counting cube, a block, a rock, a sponge, and so on. Close the bags tightly so that children can't see inside.

Let's Get Inspired

● Take a new look. Introduce the theme with a fun looking game. Bring a beautiful feather, flower, plant, or shell to your circle for the children to observe from different viewpoints. At first, the children will name or label the object. Invite them to look again and again. "What else do you notice? Tell us about the details of what you see." They might describe the colors, shape, or size of the object. Ask the children to try looking at it from different angles. "How does it look from the side? from above? from underneath? What do you notice?" Explain that they are looking at it with the eyes of an artist who sees the many different qualities and dimensions in an object. Invite them to go further by asking them to predict what the object might feel like. "If you touched this, how do you think it would feel?" Have children share their ideas before actually touching the item to test their hypotheses. Introduce a new object every day or so. This will give children an opportunity to use these skills with a variety of things.

- Sing a song of seeing. It is always wonderful when you add a song to your circle time activities. You can use the familiar tune of "Sing a Song of Sixpence" with these new words:

  Sing a song of seeing.
  I'm looking up and down.
  I see many things here: red, blue and brown.
  When I point to one thing,
  Tell me what you see.
  Isn't this a happy way
  To look and see with me?

- Sing the song and point to an object. Ask a child, "What do you see? How would you describe it?" Then sing it again, and have the first child point to something for the next child to see and describe. Continue in this manner, letting all of the children participate.

Let's Go!

- Children will want to get a chance to look at the special object from circle time. Make it available at an activity table so that they can examine it in many different ways. Ask, "Can you look at it like you are an artist? What would you draw or paint if you were an artist?" Provide drawing paper and art materials for children to make their own representations of what they see.

- Once children have observed something artistically, they can then look at the same object scientifically! Provide magnifiers, a flashlight, and measuring tape for exploring the same object with a scientist's eye. Ask, "What do you wonder about this object? What do you notice when you shine the flashlight through it? Will light shine through it? What do you see with the magnifier that you didn't see before?" The children can dictate their findings for you to write on chart paper. Try doing these two steps—art and science—with each new object you present.

- What is in the bag? Play a guessing game without sight. Children love to use their minds to guess. In a small group, give each child a bag and explain that it has a secret object inside. Have them look inside their bag to see, feel, and explore their object without showing anyone else. Then, the other children can ask questions to guess what is in the bag without seeing it or touching it. You may have to help them get started. They might ask, "What does it feel like?" "What shape is it?" "What color is it?" "How do you use it?" After the first few tries, the children will learn how to ask the questions and will enjoy the fun of guessing what is inside without seeing or touching. Continue this game with other groups of children until everyone has had a turn guessing and offering hints.

Expanding the Understanding

- Go for a silent "looking" walk. We frequently talk when we take walks with children. What would happen if we walked without talking and just looked—really looked? Explain that this is a silent walk, and invite the children to use their eyes. Invite them to look for surprises and point to them if they want to share. Try stopping along the way to just sit and look. Or, try stretching out on the grass to look at the sky. When you get back to the classroom, talk about what you saw on your silent walk that you have never noticed before.

● Play an object-permanence guessing game. Object permanence is one of the important ways that children use the sense of sight to build inference skills. It's the understanding that an object still exists, even when we can't see it. Use a cloth or scarf to partially cover an object. Ask the children to guess what it is just by seeing the small part shown. If they have trouble, show a bit more of the object by moving the scarf. Eventually uncover the item to confirm their guess. Try a variety of objects that are less and less recognizable.

Seeing with All My Senses

Do we only see with our eyes? Actually young children are excellent at using all of their senses to perceive the world around them. By expanding the viewpoint, we invite children to see beyond the two most commonly used senses of sight and hearing.

Learning Skills

Observing and comparing

Sorting and classifying

Labeling

Predicting

Sensory motor skills

Deduction

Problem solving

Materials

Poster board or whiteboard

Markers

Pillow case or cloth bag

Variety of interesting items of different shapes, textures, and sizes

Drawing paper

Large crayons with paper removed

An unusual fruit, such as mango or pomegranate

Variety of materials of different textures, such as burlap, cotton, bubble wrap, corrugated card-board, sandpaper, feathers, and velvet

Items with interesting smells

Several small screw-top plastic containers

Cotton balls

Essences, such as vanilla, lemon, almond, peppermint, chocolate, lavender, and so on

Glue sticks or glue

Safety scissors

Paper cups

Water in different temperatures: hot (but not too hot), warm, cool, and cold

Variety of objects to look through, such as nonbreakable binoculars, goggles, paper tubes, kaleido-scopes, or color paddles

Variety of foods made with apples, such as juice, applesauce, cider, vinegar, and dried apples

Feely box or shoe box with hole cut into the side.

Ahead of Time

Make scent materials by placing a few drops of essences on cotton balls. You can also use different soaps and perfumes.

Let's Get Inspired

- Sing a senses song. It is helpful to get this topic started with a song that relates the senses to the corresponding parts of the body. You can use the tune of "The Farmer in the Dell" to sing these words.

  > *I use my eyes to see.* (point to eyes)
  > *I use my eyes to see.*
  > *When I look around,*
  > *I see* (name something visible from the circle).
  > *I use my eyes to see.*

- After you have sung this song several times, move on to less familiar senses. For example:

  > *I use my fingers to touch.* (wiggle fingers)
  > *I use my fingers to touch.*
  > *When I feel around,*
  > *I touch* (name something reachable from the circle).
  > *I use my fingers to touch.*

- The children can reach out and touch something near them and describe what they feel.

- Play a touch-and-tell descriptive word game. Words are another way we experience our senses. Try this game with each of the senses of touch, smell and taste. You will be building vocabulary as you expand children's experience. Start with touch. Bring in a variety of textures, fabrics, and materials for children to touch and talk about. Pass around the first piece, and ask children to tell how they think it feels. Write their words on chart paper or whiteboard. Continue with other textures. On other days, try interesting smells and tastes!

- Explore something delicious! Your circle time can be just as yummy as snack. How can you find out about something even if you don't know what it is called? Use your senses! Bring in an unusual food or fruit such as a mango or pomegranate to share with children. Start by asking children to describe what they see. Does it look like another fruit or food they know? Invite the children to look at it, smell it, feel it, and eventually taste it.

Let's Go!

Let's be artists and scientists as we explore the senses with observation and comparison skills. These activities can be repeated throughout the week. Children gain more and more knowledge when they explore an activity several times.

- The art technique of making rubbings is a perfect combination of art and science. Normally we focus on the process of rubbing by placing a piece of paper over an object that has a texture and shape and rubbing the paper with a crayon to make a print of the texture. Try focusing on the objects first before you pass out the crayons and paper. This will encourage children to sort and classify the objects and to explore the many different textures they feel. Then, pass out the crayons and paper as a means of making an artistic recording of their exploration into texture.

- Explorations with temperature are an interesting way to experiment with the sense of touch. You can use cups of water in differing temperatures. Try cups of water representing hot (but not too hot), warm, cool, and cold. Have children close their eyes and touch inside the cups. Ask, "Which is the warmest?" "Which is the coolest?" "Can you arrange the cups in a sequence from warmest to coolest?"

- How does smell make you feel? Use the collected sets of scents for the children's exploration into the emotion and mood that the scent inspires. Lemon might make them feel happy and sunny while mint might make them feel quiet and calm. There are no wrong answers here, just their creative ideas. Write their ideas down on chart paper for easy reference and vocabulary building.

- Create a simple smell-matching game by placing a variety of odiferous items under cotton balls in small screw-top plastic containers. Make two of each, and color-code the bottoms with markers. Challenge the children to find the matching scents. They can check to see if they are correct by looking at the color coding.

- Many foods look similar but taste very different. Invite children to notice the similarities and differences among foods such as sugar and salt, water and white vinegar, peanut butter and almond butter, lemon and grapefruit, and powdered sugar and flour. Use clean spoons for a tiny taste of each.

Expanding the Understanding

- Focus children's attention on the sense of sight by providing all kinds of things for them to look through. Nonbreakable binoculars, goggles, paper tubes, kaleidoscopes, even color paddles all add to a child's-eye view of the world. Provide paper for children to draw what they see.

- Set out an apple taste test with all kinds of foods made with apples, such as juice, applesauce, cider, vinegar, and dried apples. Create a large graph for children to vote with either a smiley face or a frown face for each item tasted. Which is the favorite apple item? Which got the fewest votes?

- Bring in a box with things to feel. This will heighten children's experience of touch. Change the items daily. Pose a problem at group time for the children to solve: "Can you guess what is inside the box today without looking? How do you know?"

How I Interact with the World— Understanding the Needs and Feelings of Ourselves and Others

The best and most beautiful things in the world cannot be seen or even touched. They must be felt with the heart.

—Helen Keller, American author, lecturer

Young children are at a stage in development when they are able to look out into the world and see that others have needs and feelings, too. This is a huge leap because it means that children are not only seeing the similarities and differences in others but are now feeling them as well. As children develop more language skills, they become better able to express what they feel and need and can then reflect on how others might feel. These skills are essential to developing a global awareness because it is only when we can empathize with others that we can truly be a member of the global community. All living beings have needs, from the most basic—food, clothing, and shelter—to the emotional needs of self-awareness, acceptance, and independence.

In this section, we will look at these needs from a linguistic, social and scientific point of view.

The activities start by looking at the child and then expand to look at the needs and feelings of others. When we care about others and ourselves, we build a supportive global community of kindness and compassion that meets the needs of all.

Let's take a look at these topics:

- Roles
- Verbal communication
- Nonverbal communication
- Helping
- Water
- A place to live
- Safety and health
- Food
- Animals' needs

I Am, You Are

Dramatic play is fertile ground for developing the language of expressing feelings and needs. When children explore many different roles, they develop an awareness of the social function of language—both spoken and written. As children learn these ways of communicating, they also learn how to connect with the larger world community. In this activity, children will begin to develop linguistic skills for communication and dialogue.

Learning Skills

Expressive language

Social interaction

Role playing

Listening

Labeling and writing

Materials

Poster board or whiteboard

Cardboard or card stock

Drawing paper, crayons, and markers

Safety scissors

Glue sticks and/or glue

Magazines

Playdough or clay

Craft sticks (optional)

Photographs of children and their families (optional)

Digital camera or smartphone camera

Boxes

Objects and clothing for dramatic play

Print materials related to the dramatic play

Ahead of Time

- Invite children's families to share photos of family members. These would be ones that they don't mind being cut and pasted. You can also use your smartphone or digital camera to take photos of children and family to print.

- Cut out photos of people from magazines.

- Create prop boxes with objects and clothing children can use for thematic role play. Themes might include restaurant, veterinarian, or grocery store. Be sure to include print materials in each box that will encourage both prereading and writing.

Let's Get Inspired

Children love to be recognized in your circle-time meetings. It is a way for them to feel respected both as individuals and as members of the group. In these circle interactions, we will celebrate all the different roles and names we have.

- Start by playing with the many different names and labels that can describe us. Model by saying your name: "I am Ms. Ellen." Ask the children to say their names using "I am . . ." to start. Ask the children, "Do you have another name?" The children may like to share their last name or a family nickname with the group. Share your nickname, too: "I am Ellen Church Mouse!"

- Now invite the children to think about another name or label that describes them. For example, they might say, "I am a girl. I am a sister. I am four years old. I am Susie's cousin. I am Rama's friend." This can be a list for each child or a class list that you make on chart paper and add to each day during these investigations. Pretty soon you will have a great "I am" list to refer to!

- Create an "I Like, We Like" chart. The next logical step after discussing our names can be a discussion of what we like and don't like. Use your whiteboard or chart paper to make a two-part chart. In the left column, list all the things the children like. On the right side, list the things they dislike. It might be helpful to start with something concrete, such as foods they like and dislike. Be sure to write the child's name with the words for his like and dislike. If possible, draw a simple rebus drawing to illustrate the words. Children will love to refer to the chart using their names and the images.

- Talk about preferences throughout the study. Each day, introduce a new topic to discuss the children's thoughts and feelings. Remember, there are no wrong responses. This will encourage children to express their interests, needs, and feelings without fear. Topics might include class activities. "How do you feel about story time? snack time? block play? painting? outdoor play?" You may even want to ask, "How could (name of activity) be better? What would you change?"

Let's Go!

- Make photo dolls or puppets. This is a great way to explore the different roles of people in the community. Provide photographs of people from magazines and online. Show the children how to cut around the images and glue them on cardboard. They can stand the cardboard dolls in a small piece of playdough or clay. Children can use craft sticks to make the photos into puppets.

- Use the dolls or puppets to create little role plays. Invite the children to choose a doll and speak for it. "What does it want to say to the other one?" Children might like to invent their own stories about the dolls.

- Introduce themed prop boxes. Children learn about roles in society by experimenting with different dramatic play themes and roles. Show children the objects in a prop box, and invite them to guess what the items are used for. Then send the children off to the dramatic play area to create their own roles. It is very important to allow children to figure this out themselves. If you stand back and watch supportively, you will notice which children are leaders and which are followers. If possible, use photography to record some of the interactions.

- Create *I Am . . .* books. Children may like to create personal books based on the "I am" lists they have contributed to in circle time. They can make individual books with words and illustrations for each "I am" phrase, or they can put them all together in a class big book.

Expanding the Understanding

- Experiment with role playing in movement games. These are great to take outside to the playground or to do in a large, open indoor space. For example, you can play with how the types of shoes people wear affect the way they move. Put on some music for children to move to as they pretend to wear different types of shoes: work boots, ice skates, slippers, toe shoes, high heels, and skis. Stop the music periodically to change the "shoe" and the movement. Play the game another time with different types of hats workers wear!

- Play telephone! This old favorite is still a hit with kids. You can choose a simple word to whisper and pass around the circle back to the beginning. Then move to a phrase or sentence. What comes out at the other end?

- Try a new Red Light, Green Light game that uses the photo cards of people that the children created. Have the children stand in a line across from you. When you say *green light,* show a photo. They have to move like that person would move. When you say *red light,* they stop and wait for the next image to imitate.

So Many Messages

Communication in all its many forms is key in assisting children in learning how to transmit information and express feelings and ideas. In the global community, the ability to communicate is essential to peaceful and productive interactions. At this rich time of literacy development, young children need to see their oral messages translated into print. This prepares them for crucial reading and writing tasks that lie ahead in school and in the wide world. The children will begin to develop an understanding of the many ways to communicate feelings, needs, and ideas.

Learning Skills

Expressive language

Dictation

Spoken word–written word correlation

Drawing

Prereading

Prewriting

Materials

Drawing paper

Tape

Markers, crayons

Chart paper or whiteboard

Envelopes

Rubber stamps and stamp pads (optional)

Grocery-store circulars

Safety scissors

Glue sticks

Small pads

Pencils

Photos from magazines of street signs

Library pockets or envelopes

Basket (optional)

Ahead of Time

- Cut the drawing paper into 8-inch squares.
- Create a message center for the classroom using a low bulletin board or room divider outfitted with library pockets or envelopes for each child.

Let's Get Inspired

Children love to see their words written down. It is one of the most important ways we can validate their feelings and ideas. You can introduce the idea of sending and receiving messages in your circle time with songs and games. This will get children involved and interested in the topic.

- Start with a song. The tune of the old nursery song "A Tisket, A Tasket" is perfect for this theme.

    A tisket, a tasket,
    A green and yellow basket.
    Wrote a letter to my friend, (pretend to hold up an envelope)
    And on the way I mailed it. (pretend to drop it into a mailbox)
    I mailed it, I mailed it,
    And on the way I mailed it.
    A little boy picked it up
    And put it in his pocket. (pretend to put the envelope in your pocket)

- Share a message with the class. One of the best ways to talk about all kinds of messages is to share a real or pretend one with children. You can bring in a note a family member wrote to you or a letter you received in the mail. Children will be fascinated to learn something about you this way! Then show them a note you wrote for them. This can be a simple message about the day or week ahead. Start making a message from you a part of your meeting time every morning!

- Introduce dictation. Young children are at the perfect stage to discover the art and joy of dictation. It is through this simple process that children make the connection between their spoken words and written words. Start with something simple and silly. Ask the children to suggest their favorite (or silliest, happiest, funniest) word. As each child says a word, write it slowly on chart paper or the whiteboard. Spell the word as you write it. Add the child's name next to his word, for pride of ownership. Read the words together.

Let's Go!

After the children have been introduced to the fun of sending messages, you can take the concept into all your learning centers.

- Let's make shopping lists! Bring in your own shopping list and some grocery-store circulars to show the children how they can write their own. They may want to cut out the items they want to put on their lists. You could write the words for the items, and they could copy them or trace them to add to their lists. Put these materials in the dramatic play area along with small pads and pencils, envelopes, and stickers (for stamps) to provide children with ongoing opportunities to write shopping lists and letters.

- Add signs to the block area. Signs are another way of sending a message. A sign might say "Stop" or "Be Careful" or "Stay Out." Show children photos of different road signs, and help them make signs for their block buildings.

- Create a message center in the writing area. You can involve the children in creating the board by asking them to write their names on the pockets. Place small pieces of paper and markers in the area so the children can write and draw messages at any time. Children can freely leave messages in each other's message pockets throughout the day.

- In the art area, show children how to make their own envelopes. You will need 8-inch square paper to do this. Show the children how to fold three corners into the center to make a pocket. Tape the corners in place, and use the fourth one as the tongue of the envelope. What will you send?

- Be a class secretary! Set up "appointments" during free-play time for the children to come to you and offer their dictation of a letter or thought or feeling. This works well with a computer so that children can watch their words appear on the screen as you type them. Print the messages out for illustration and sending!

Expanding the Understanding

- Play a circle game. Use the song "A Tisket, A Tasket" in a game similar to Duck, Duck, Goose. Ask the children to sit in a circle. Have one child skip or walk around the outside of the circle carrying a basket with an envelope inside. On the line about dropping the letter, the child drops the envelope in back of a child, and they both race around the circle to get back to the space (and the envelope) first.

- Write book reviews. Share the children's thoughts and feelings about the books you are reading by asking them to dictate their review of a current book. You can write their thoughts on chart paper and then have children "sign" it.

- Send a note home. Children may like to show off their note-writing skills by writing a note home to their families once a week. It is a great way to keep in touch with families, and they will be impressed to receive a handwritten note.

Puppets Speak!

Cultures around the world use a variety of puppets to communicate through storytelling. Often children will feel more comfortable expressing a thought, feeling, or need through a puppet's voice than through their own. By using the platform of a puppet, children can express both fanciful and real communications. Let the puppets speak! The children will begin to use expressive language as they create roles and communication with puppets.

Learning Skills

Expressive language

Role playing

Social interaction

Spatial relationships

Listening

Following directions

Story sequence

Materials

Recycled materials for puppet making, such as socks, paper tubes and plates, craft sticks, and decorative objects

Tape and glue sticks

Cardboard or card stock

Images from stories such as *Goldilocks and the Three Bears, The Three Little Pigs,* or *Three Billy Goats Gruff*

Water-soluble markers

Crayons

Nontoxic, washable lipstick and eyebrow pencil

Magazines

Large cardboard box

Safety Scissors

Ahead of Time

Create puppets of characters from familiar stories such as *Goldilocks and the Three Bears, The Three Little Pigs,* or *Three Billy Goats Gruff.* You can download images or cut up a worn old paperback book. Glue the images on cardboard and attach them to craft sticks so that children can use them to tell their own versions of the story.

Let's Get Started!

There is something magical about a puppet. Whether it is a stuffed animal, a paper bag, or just a hand speaking to them, children are captivated by the interaction. In this section we will explore many ways to use puppets to encourage verbal expression and communication.

- Before circle time, secretly draw a face on the side of your hand with lipstick and eye liner. Keep your hand hidden as you start the circle. Then announce, "I have a new friend. He would like to join us in singing our circle-time song this morning. Do you want to meet him?" Slowly take your hand out, and move your thumb joint up and down to make the puppet look like it is talking. Start the song right away without any discussion. After singing, talk about your new puppet friend. Invite children to ask it questions and welcome him to the circle!

- Share a favorite story. Use a story such as *Goldilocks and the Three Bears* to introduce character puppets. Show one puppet at a time, and ask the children to suggest who the character might be. Invite them to think about what the story might be. As you add the puppets, the children will naturally guess. Ask them to help you tell the story using the puppets. "What happens first?" "What does Goldilocks do?" "What happens next?" "What does Goldilocks say about the porridge?" Don't worry about the story being perfect. Just enjoy the story they create with the puppets.

Let's Go!

- Let the children make their own hand puppets. Show them how to carefully use nontoxic washable lipstick and eye liner to draw a face on one of their hands. Then, invite them to choose a partner to have a "face-to-face" conversation. They can ask each other questions or tell something about themselves. Wash hands before going to another activity!

- Create a story time puppet theater. Invite children to help you cut up and decorate a large cardboard box for a puppet theater in the language or literacy area of the room. Over time, provide different sets of puppets for children to use in their own retelling of stories.

- Make family puppets. Children will enjoy looking through magazines for photos of people to make into stick puppets. They may like to look for mommies, daddies, sisters, brothers, or other family members. Show them how to back the photo with cardboard and glue the image on a stick. Children can use the puppets in the theater to tell their own stories. If possible, record some of their shows to share with the families.

Expanding the Understanding

- Play Puppet May I. Use a classroom puppet friend to play a variation on the game of Mother May I out on the playground. The child with the puppet stands about twenty feet away from the other children. The more the merrier for this game! The puppet gives specific directions to each child with the goal of the children reaching the puppet. The puppet might say, "Jessie, you may take three steps sideways." Then the child asks, "Puppet may I?" The puppet says yes or no. If a child forgets to ask, then he has to give up his turn! This is a great game for listening and following directions.

- Create family puppets at home. Extend the activity by sending a family puppet-making kit home. Families can use old photos of themselves or take new photos. Children will enjoy bringing their family puppets back to school for show and tell. Encourage them to tell a story with their puppet families.

Communicating without Words

Children are great communicators. They learn to express their needs and feelings from infancy onward. In the early years, children often do not have words to express how they are feeling or what they need. They quickly find ways to use their movements, sounds, and expressions to tell you what is going on. This innate understanding of communication is wonderful to celebrate as we explore how we feel about the world and then communicate those feelings and needs to others. Plus, the ability to communicate nonverbally can be quite helpful when connecting with people who do not speak the same language!

Learning Skills

Nonverbal communication

Reading symbols and pictures

Storytelling with images

Creative movement

Materials

Magazines

Images of signs

Safety scissors

Glue sticks and/or paste

Chart paper or whiteboard

Paper

Markers and crayons

Poster board or oak tag

Examples of wordless books

Collect images of signs to share with children. These can be downloaded from an image search or found in magazines or books. If possible, find signs from many different countries.

Let's Get Inspired

Your circle time can be noisy or silent or something in between. Let's experiment with communicating with the group using a variety of methods beyond words.

- Use welcome gestures. Capture children's interest and inspire communication by inviting them to circle time with welcoming gestures instead of words. You might want to wave and point the way to circle time. Once they are there, you can welcome them with a smile, a hand shake, a pinky wave—whatever you like. Interestingly, children often are so surprised by the lack of words that they follow your directions well.

- Talk about it. After children have arrived, ask them what they thought you were meaning with your gestures. "How did you know what I was saying? I didn't say any words." Help children understand that they can "say" something without speaking.

- Give the children a few phrases to experiment with. Ask them to show how they can communicate one without speaking. For example, try, "I love you," "Be quiet," or "Good work."

- Use the tune of "The Farmer in the Dell" to sing a hello song. Start with their hands, and then ask them to think of other movements or body parts for saying hello!

    My hand says hello. (wave)
    My hand says hello.
    Every time I see my friends,
    My hand says hello.

- You can also invite children to "say" something with a movement and ask the others to guess what they are communicating.

- At another circle time, talk to the children with sounds instead of words. They will be surprised to find they know what you are saying without the words they know. You can use exaggerated facial expressions and movements to "talk." For example, you might say sounds such as *blerk, bick, burb, burb* as you point to a story you are going to read.

Let's Go!

Young children learn to read a story being conveyed in pictures long before they read words. Let's focus on building those literacy skills with activities that invite children to tell stories without words.

- Create a wordless book display. Collect a wide variety of wordless books for children to examine and read. Place these in your literacy area with a sign "Every Picture Tells a Story." Encourage the children to visit the area often to read the books on their own. Children can also take turns being the "reader" and telling the story to other children.

- Children can explore the concept of pictures telling a story with a simple art activity. Provide paper and drawing materials for children to draw a picture to tell the story of something that happened at home or on a trip. Encourage them to add as much detail as they can. When the story picture is complete, ask the children to tell you their story by looking at the picture. Write their words on a separate sheet of paper or cardstock so they can be displayed along with the drawing.

- Signs are another way that we communicate without speaking. Show the children a variety of signs, and have them tell you what they think the signs say. Explore signs from different countries. The signs might have words in another language, but the children will notice that they can "read" them using the images.

- The children may be inspired to make their own signs based on the ones they have been studying. Provide poster board and markers, magazine pictures, and glue sticks to let them create signs for the classroom and for the dramatic play or block area.

- Use collage to create a wordless book. Young children may find it easier and more fun to cut out pictures instead of drawing them. For example, children may like to use animal magazines to create a story about an animal. Provide a large sheet of drawing paper folded in half to create a four-page book. Children can add additional pages with another sheet of folded paper. Read the book at circle time!

Expanding the Understanding

- Make movement signs for outdoor play. Lines are often used to wordlessly demonstrate a place to go or a way to move. Children can help you create cards to use on the playground. Each card can represent a type of movement. What sort of line shows hopping, skipping, running, or tiptoeing?

- Try telling a story while children listen with their eyes closed. This allows them to "see" the illustrations in their own way. You can make up a story with vivid images or retell a familiar story. After the story, invite children to share what they "saw"!

- Whisper a phrase for a child to demonstrate and for the others to guess. Explore movements such as digging a hole, hammering a nail, cutting, raking, eating, and painting.

Who Needs Me, and How Can I Help?

Young children naturally want to help. In fact, in the early years, children love to help with simple kitchen and household chores. Helping means children feel important and confident that they know what to do. But children can't fulfill all their needs by themselves. In a very simple way, children are beginning to realize that they need the help of others, particularly family and friends.

Encourage children to explore their own needs and the needs of those around them. These are the first steps to empathy in the world community.

Learning Skills

Social interaction

Expressive language

Self-regulation

Literacy

Materials

Drawing paper

Markers and crayons

Gummed paper

Scissors

Photo album

Digital camera (optional)

Ahead of Time

Cut 1-inch-wide paper strips out of gummed paper for paper-chain making.

Let's Get Inspired

Your circle time is one of the best times and places to build an awareness of the needs and feelings of others. This essential time of community provides the children with the opportunity to explore how they can help each other. With songs, games, and discussions, your circle is the heart of your classroom community.

- Start the day with an awareness of each other with "Headline News." Sharing a class full of personal news can take much more time than young children have the patience to listen to. Try inviting children to share the headlines of their news instead of the entire story. Demonstrate how a headline is a short sentence or statement: "I saw a deer on the way to school this morning!" or "Ms. Ellen Sees Deer on the Way to School."

- Sing a song of friends helping. Turn "The Farmer in the Dell" into a helping song. Tape a piece of paper to the floor. Ask for a volunteer to stand in the middle of the circle next to the paper, and hand her a crayon. Encourage that child to draw a simple image of her choosing on the paper. Start singing. The child in the middle chooses someone to come help her, then that child can choose someone, and so on. Each child helps by adding to the drawing.

> *The friend in the middle,*
> *The friend in the middle.*
> *Hi-ho we help you so!*
> *The friend in the middle.*
> *The friend helps a friend,*
> *The friend helps a friend.*
> *Hi-ho we help you so!*
> *The friend helps a friend.*

- Talk about helping. Ask the children about ways they can help others. "What do you do at home to help?" "What do you do at school?" Remember to also talk about getting help when we need it. You can give an example of how you might need help and who might help you. Ask the children what kinds of help they might need and who would provide it.

Let's Go!

In the different centers of your classroom, explore the concept of helping each other. You can keep the theme of helping as a focus for several weeks.

- Write a cooperative class book. Ask the children, "What are friends for?" Use this as the focus of the book. Provide drawing materials and paper for them to design their own pages about what they think friends are for. If possible, add photos of friends to the book, and place all the pages together in a large photo album to use at story time.

- Make an artistic group creation. You can celebrate helping each other by creating a giant paper chain. Use strips of gummed paper strips that will stick together when pressed. Ask, "How can we help each other make a chain as long as the rug?" "How can we make one as long as the hall? Let's work together and see." As a group, decide where to hang the chain, then work together to do so.

- Your block area is a great place to work with the concept of helping each other. You can experiment by asking each child to add one block at a time to a construction project. There may be problems they have to solve together, such as the structure falling down. But this is part of the helping concept that is so important for children to learn. If possible, take progressive photos of the construction project to show how the building is formed through cooperative effort.

- My family needs me. Ask the children, "Who needs you in your family?" How does your mother or father need you? How do your sister, brother, or grandparents need you?" Invite the children to think about what each of their family members need them for—everything from a hug and kiss to clearing the table. Children can work over many days to make a personal book titled *My Family Needs ME*. Each page can show their drawings and dictation for how their parents, siblings, grandparents, and pets need them. Parents will love to receive these books as gifts.

Expanding the Understanding

- Children love to help each other learn a new skill, such as hopping on one foot or snapping fingers or spinning a yo-yo. Set up a time each day for a child to share a skill she would like to help others learn. Then be sure to offer practice time on the playground or during free-play time.

- Make a helping coupon book. After a discussion of how they can help out at home, children can make a coupon book to give to family members filled with ideas for ways to help. There could be coupon for getting up on time or cleaning their room!

- Take helping outside! Play a circle game called Have You Seen My Friend? It is similar to Duck, Duck, Goose. One child stands in the center of the circle and secretly chooses someone in the circle as the "friend." Then the child in the center spins around and points to someone in the circle and describes the friend. "Have you seen my friend? My friend is wearing red." The child on the outside of the circle gets one guess. If that child is wrong, the center child spins again. But if she guesses correctly, the player chases the friend around the circle back to his place. If she catches him, he is "it," but if not the searcher starts again with a new friend!

Every Living Thing Needs Water

Noticing the universal need for water is a great way to help children recognize how all living things have similar needs and life functions. By studying the ways humans, animals, and plants need water, the complex world out there becomes more understandable and even manageable. Let's start with the element of water and see how much we need it.

Learning Skills

Observation

Hypothesizing

Experimentation

Recording findings

Materials

Mini bottles of spring water (Note: These are available at the dollar store.)

Potting soil

Seeds, such as marigold or green bean

Styrofoam egg cartons or plastic cups

Nature magazines

Chart paper or whiteboard

Markers

Sand table or bin filled with sand

Digging toys

Nonbreakable water pitchers

Orange juice concentrate

Powdered milk

Dried and fresh fruit, such as grapes and raisins

Digital camera (optional)

Let's Get Inspired

Most children don't notice their need for water, or they take the availability of water for granted. These activities are designed to help children see how all living things need water, just like they do!

- Start with a water song such as "Three Little Fishies" to get the discussion of water going. With each verse change the word *swim* to a different word that relates to water. Try words such as *drink, splash, wash,* and *float.*

- Talk about water. You can start a conversation about water after the song. "What are the things you do with water? Do you swim, drink, splash, and wash, too?" Write the children's ideas on the whiteboard or chart paper, and put each child's name next to his idea.

- Start a conversation about the need for water. Ask, "Have you ever been thirsty? How did it feel?" "Did you ever see an animal come in from playing outside go right for the water bowl?" "What happens if you forget to water a plant?" The purpose is to help children see how we need water and how other living things do, too. Write children's ideas on chart paper or the whiteboard. This can be a list of living things that need water. Add to this throughout the study.

- Try a thirsty experiment. Invite the children to do some vigorous exercise at circle time. They could do jumping jacks, arm raises in place, circle games—anything to make them thirsty! After the exercise, invite them to notice how they feel. They might notice their heart rates and how their mouths and throats feel. Ask, "What do you need? What would make you feel better? Why?" Offer children individual mini spring-water bottles to quench their thirst. Talk about the difference in how they feel after they have had some water. Ask, "Do dogs get thirsty like that? Who else gets thirsty?"

Let's Go!

The topic of water naturally fits with science and math explorations. But don't forget to celebrate water with stories, too.

- Water creates change. Start this activity with dry sand in the sandbox or a bin. Children can explore pouring, scooping, and building with the dry sand. Ask, "Can you build a sandcastle with dry sand? What do you need?" Have them slowly add water to the mixture, and discuss how the sand changes. Ask, "What can you do with wet sand that you couldn't with dry?" Children may like to explore making rivers and ponds in the sand. Record the children's findings on chart paper divided into two columns: "Dry Sand" and "Wet Sand."

- Children are often surprised to find out that there is water in many things they eat and drink. Set up an experiment to demonstrate this. Explain that many things they drink and eat are made of water. Ask the children to help you add water to make orange juice from concentrate and to make milk from powdered milk. Ask, "Did you know you were drinking water when you drink your milk?" Compare dried and fresh fruits. Grapes and raisins are good examples. Explain that the only difference is that the water is taken out of the grape. Ask the children to notice how the fruits look different and taste different. The children may like to experiment with dehydrating fresh grapes into raisins, too!

- Perform a Goldilocks experiment. Have the children experiment with seeds or seedlings. Give some too much water. Give some too little water. And give some just the right amount of water. What happens to the seeds with too much or too little? Children can make field drawings of their work as they observe their seedlings over time. Plants need water, but not too much!

- Write water stories. Children will enjoy looking through nature magazines for photos to use to create a collage of a water storybook. They might choose photos and make up a story about what they see. Or they can use the photos to create a story about why we need water.

Expanding the Understanding

- Take a water walk. It is important for children to see the way water is used and found in their environment. Take a walk around the inside of school and look for where they find water and how it is being used. "How do we use water in the bathroom? the kitchen?" Then go outside to look for places where water is naturally collecting or where water is used. If possible, use a digital camera to take photos to record their findings for a chart or book.

- Make a water clock. Invite the children to think about how they use water at different times of the day. Draw a large circle with spokes coming out for different parts of the day. (It will look something like a sun.) Starting at the top, ask the children to brainstorm how they use water when they first get up. Write this on one of the spokes. Continue throughout the day, looking at water use until bedtime.

- Send a copy of the water clock home. Parents will enjoy making a home version. Ask them to fill out a water clock with the family and return it to school with their child.

We All Need a Place to Live

A place of shelter is a universal need for all beings. Children and families, animals and birds—they all need a place to go. Children will begin to develop an understanding of the need for shelter and the many ways to create it.

Learning Skills

Observation

Comparison

Construction

Problem solving

Drawing

Writing

Self-reflection

Materials

Sticky note paper

Tempera paint

Paintbrushes

A large assortment of boxes

Recycled materials, such as paper tubes, plates, yarn, fabric, and so on

Small brown paper lunch bags

Glue and glue sticks

Safety scissors

Drawing paper

Markers

Chart paper or whiteboard

Magazines

Clay and/or sand

Sheets and scarves

Let's Get Inspired

The conversations and activities you provide in the circle invite children to think about their own needs and the needs of others. For this theme, let's talk about shelter and homes.

● Introduce the concept of shelter with a personal story. You might share a story about getting caught in the rain or a simple story about being comfortable at home. You might begin by saying, "I want to tell you about a time I was glad to have a shelter to go home to. One day . . . ." After the story, invite the children to share something special about their homes. It could be who lives there or what the home looks like. Note: Be sensitive that some children may not have something to share. You know your group best. Adapt this activity as needed.

● Create a home chart. Everybody's home is different. Some are big buildings with many families living there; some are small with just one family living in it. The people inside make a dwelling a home. Create a group chart showing the number of children who live in a one-family home, two-family home, or three- (or more) family home. Write *One Family, Two Families,* and *Three or More Families* across the top of chart paper or the white board. Children can use a sticky note to "vote" for the type of home they live in. Which type of home do most people live in?

● Sing a home song to the familiar tune of "BINGO." This will help children start thinking of houses, homes, and shelter. You can add verses for animals. Where does a bird live? a cow? Add them to the song!

> *There was a child who had a family*
> *And lived inside a house so.*
> *H-O-U-S-E, H-O-U-S-E, H-O-U-S-E*
> *A house was where they lived so.*
>
> *There was a child who had a family*
> *And lived in an apartment.*
> *H-O-M-E, H-O-M-E, H-O-M-E*
> *An apartment was where they lived so.*
>
> *There was a cow who had a family*
> *And lived inside a barn so.*
> *B-A-R-N, B-A-R-N, B-A-R-N*
> *A barn was where they lived so.*

- Talk about how animals find shelter. Animals as well as people need to have shelter from the weather. Ask, "Where do you go when it rains or snows?" "Where do you think the bugs, birds, and butterflies go when it rains?" Be open to children's ideas even if they don't seem logical. Write them down for exploration later.

- Talk about the weather. It is natural to talk about weather when talking about shelter and houses. You can focus on weather watching during this theme to see when people and creatures might need to take shelter. If possible, show photos of different kinds of weather. You can show a hot sunny day, a snowy day, and a rainstorm. Invite the children to brainstorm the kind of shelter needed for each of the different kinds of weather.

Let's Go!

Let's explore the many ways to create shelter.

- Paint your house. Children may like to go to the art area to paint a large representation of their home. Invite them to think about what color it is and what materials were used to make it. Display these in a bulletin board titled: "A House Is a House for Me!" (based on the book by Mary Ann Hoberman).

- There are many kinds of homes. Children will enjoy going through nature and travel magazines to find photos of many different kinds of homes around the world. They can collage these into a class book. Help the children notice that some homes are made very differently than the ones in their town.

- Create block houses. Use some images of homes around the world to inspire children's block building. Children can glue photos on poster board and hang them in the block area for creative exploration. Try to take photos of their structures to display next to the inspiration photo.

- What can you do with boxes? Children love boxes of all sizes. Bring in a wide variety of boxes for children to experiment with making shelters and homes. How many ways can you build a shelter with boxes?

- What can you do with sheets? Not all homes are solid like a box. Some are open and made of cloth. Provide children with a variety of sheets and scarves to create a shelter in the classroom or outside. How will you make your shelter stay up?

- How can you build with clay and sand? Children may also like to explore building shelters and homes in the sand table with both clay and sand.

Expanding the Understanding

- Take a neighborhood walk. If possible, take a walk around the school neighborhood to examine the many different types of shelter in your area. The children may notice some are made of wood, brick, stucco, or stone. Point out different types of buildings, from dwellings to stores and offices. How do they provide shelter?

- "Paint" the school! A classic activity for outdoor play is "painting" with water and big brushes. Have a school "paint-in" outside on your playground. Children will love to see how the water changes the color of the building for a while!

- Send home a project! Fill a brown paper lunch bag with a variety of recycled materials, such as paper tubes, small boxes, paper plates, and so on, that can be used for building. Present a problem for the family to solve. How can you use these materials to create a shelter? Who might live there?

We All Need to Feel Safe and Healthy

Keeping healthy and safe are important needs and feelings of all people. This universal theme invites children to notice their own needs and the tools and rules we use to keep everyone safe and healthy.

Learning Skills

Observation

Comparison

Prediction

Dramatization

Sorting and classifying

Gross motor skills

Problem solving

Materials

Drawing paper

Markers

Glue sticks

Safety scissors

An assortment of health tools, such as a toothbrush and toothpaste, a comb and brush, a sun hat, a spoon, a cup, and so on

Magazines

Chart paper or whiteboard

Large plastic hoops

Balance beam

Balls

Buckets

Ahead of Time

- Collect a variety of health tools that the children will use to sort and match.
- Create an obstacle course outside using a variety of materials, such as large plastic hoops, a beam, and buckets.

Let's Get Inspired

To some children, the topic of health and safety might seem boring, but with some fun discussions and activities at circle time, you can inspire children to dive into this theme.

- How do you stay safe? Begin a discussion of safety by asking children to brainstorm their ideas of the ways they stay safe. You might need to give them situations to discuss. For example you might ask, "How do you stay safe on the way to school? at school? after school?" Record their ideas on a chart that can be illustrated during activity time.

- Sing a song of safety. You can use the tune of "This Is the Way" to make a safety song with some of the children's safety brainstorms.

    This is the way we cross the street. (look to the right and to the left)
    This is the way we cross the street,
    Cross the street, cross the street, cross the street.
    This is the way we cross the street,
    So we can stay healthy.

    Other verses:
    This is the way we wear a seat belt. (pretend to put a seat belt on)

    This is the way we brush our teeth. (pretend to brush teeth)

    This is the way we ask for help. (tap another person on the shoulder)

- What do we do in an emergency? Talk about the different things to do in an emergency. For example, in a fire drill, line up and walk outside with your teacher. For a real emergency, call 911. If you are approached by a stranger, never talk to or go with a stranger. Tell a grownup you know.

- Invite a health visitor. It is always helpful for children to meet a visitor in circle time. Perhaps there is a safety person at the school or a doctor, dentist, or nurse who would be willing to visit. Ahead of time, have the children brainstorm questions they would like to ask the visitor and write these on chart paper.

- Sing a "Keep Healthy" song. We know that hand washing is one of the best ways to keep from spreading germs and getting sick. The trick is to wash our hands with soap long enough for it to work—approximately twenty seconds. Sing the following lyrics to the tune of "Skip to My Lou" twice through.

> *Wash, wash, wash my hands,* (pretend to wash hands)
> *Wash, wash, wash my hands,*
> *Wash, wash, wash my hands,*
> *Wash with soap and water.*

Let's Go!

Your centers will be jumping with this theme that involves the dramatic play, blocks, art, and literacy areas of your classroom.

- Safe for babies. Children are often very interested in babies, their care, and their safety. Show children how to do a common household test of items too small to be safe for babies. Cut a paper-towel tube in half and use it as a choke-test tube. Provide a tester tube for each child and a box of items of different sizes to test. Children can sort the objects by "safe" and "not safe" for babies.

- Safe to share. Some things are safe for us to share with others, and some we don't want to share. Provide a collection of items for children to sort into the two different categories. For example, a comb, brush, hat, toothbrush, spoon, cup, fork, tissue, and whistle are non-share items. Books, toys, tools, crayons, pencils, trucks, drums, dolls, and chairs can be shared. Record the children's findings in a graph, organizing the two columns of items in straight lines. Ask the children, "Which do we have more of?"

- Set up a travel security check point. During travel is one of the main times people need to be safe. You can transform your dramatic play area into an airport, with a check-in desk, security checkpoint, boarding gate, and seats on the plane.

- Make bandage art. A fun project is to stick bandages of various shapes and sizes on a sheet of paper. Use tempera colors to paint over the bandages. When the bandages are removed, an interesting pattern results. Ask the children, "What happens when you take a bandage off a cut?"

- Bath time in the water table: Use dolls, soap, a toothbrush, a washcloth, and so on to reenact morning or evening bath time.

- Write a *Class Safety* book. The children may like to go through magazines for photos of safe and unsafe activities and objects. Talk with them about which category the activities or objects belong in and why. Invite them to create collages of the pictures to show pages for each category.

- Our safety rules: Children are often more aware of the classroom rules if they create them together. Ask children to illustrate some of the rules for the classroom with drawings. These can become safety signs around the room and building.

Expanding the Understanding

- Tour the playground for safety. Make health and safety interactive by involving children in the process. Take a safety walk around the playground to discuss potential hazards and ways to deal with them. Invite the children to collectively make safety rules for the playground.

- Make an exercise course outside. Exercise is a very important way we stay healthy and safe. Create an obstacle course in the playground with hula hoops to walk through, a beam to walk across, buckets for throwing balls into, and so on. Encourage the children to look at your outdoor play materials and make suggestions for the exercise course.

- Play Red Light, Green Light. Don't forget the classic game of Red Light, Green Light. Children can color paper plates to make the signs and can use them to play the game—even with riding toys.

- Drink water. Children can get overheated before they know it. Remind them to drink water when they are outside. You can keep chilled water bottles (labeled with the children's names) available in a cooler to create a self-service water area.

- Take imaginary field trips. Sometimes families can't get away as much as they would like. You can invite children to use creative movement and dramatics for taking imaginary trips right in your own playground! Inside the classroom, ask children where they would like to go if they could go anywhere. Write down their ideas, and have them choose a destination. Then, brainstorm ideas for what they can do to create the pretend trip to the beach or zoo—anywhere! For example, if they want to go on a camping trip, ask, "What props would we need?" "What are the types of movements we can make to show traveling to the campground, setting up the tents, and playing there?" When everything is in place, head outside to enact the trip. This dramatic-play activity can go on for days, so be open to children creatively adding to and changing the play.

Everybody Needs to Eat

Children are well aware of the need to eat. But, do they understand how eating some foods fills the need better than others? In this theme, explore the need for good food and nutrition for all people. The children will begin to develop an understanding about the need to eat healthy food.

Learning Skills

Brainstorming and discussion

Sorting and classifying

Writing

Creative expression

Materials

Chart paper or whiteboard

Markers

Cooking or food-related magazines

Paper plates and napkins

Glue sticks or glue

A variety of wheat food products, such as bread, cookies, cereal, pita, matzo, and bulgur

A variety of vegetables, such as carrots, celery, lettuce, spinach, radishes, and broccoli

Creamy salad dressing

Raisins and grapes

Sunflower seeds

Almonds or cashews

Apple slices

Ziplock storage bags (one per child)

Let's Get Inspired

You can start with general discussions and activities in your circle time that invite the children to begin thinking about their needs and the needs of others.

- Start with a song to welcome children as you start the conversation about what people need. Use the tune of "Frère Jacques" with the following words.

  > *I need you,* (point to self then someone else)
  > *I need you,*
  > *For a smile,* (smile)
  > *For a smile.*

Everyone needs you, (open arms wide)
Everyone needs you,
For a smile, (smile)
For a smile.

- Replace the word *smile* with other words that children suggest that people need, such as *hug, friend,* and so on. You can also change the words to fit a very specific need, such as needing everyone to sit down or listen. End with, "Welcome! We need you here!"

- Get children thinking and talking about what they need with general questions, such as "What do you need in the morning?" "What do you need in the afternoon?" "What do you need at night?" Make three columns on chart paper or a whiteboard, and head them with the three times of day. Write down children's ideas as they brainstorm what they need first thing in the morning, in the afternoon, and at night. Interestingly, most children will probably first think of the things needed for survival: food, water, clothing, and safety.

- Focus on food. Everyone needs to eat. What do you like to eat? What should you eat? Introduce the concept of *anytime* and *sometimes* foods. Invite children to guess what foods are good to eat anytime. Write these on chart paper. Then ask what foods are only good to eat now and then—sometimes. You may be surprised how much children already know about eating good fruits and vegetables and only eating candy, cake, and ice cream on special occasions.

Let's Go!

Of course, cooking and eating are essential to this theme. There are many spinoffs that involve math recording, creative writing, and art. Let's play with our food!

- Simply categorizing food as ones that are good sometimes and others that are good anytime helps children learn how to eat healthy. Provide the children with food photos to sort and organize. Invite the children to explain why they think some foods are only good sometimes.

- Create an *Anytime Food Alphabet Book*. The children may like to collect photos of healthy anytime foods and paste them into a simple alphabet book. They may need help finding some foods for certain letters, but you can encourage them to put in food tools as well!

- Have a wheat taste test. Children are often surprised to find out what is in some of their favorite foods. Bring in a variety of foods that contain wheat for children to taste and compare. Fasten food samples on a poster with two columns to check: like (smiley face) or don't like (frown face) stickers. Note: Make sure none of your students has a wheat allergy. before doing this activity.

- Create a veggie buffet. Invite the children to help you make a veggie salad bar for snack time. They can help you wash and prepare the vegetables and put out small containers of creamy salad dressing for dipping. Ask them, "Which veggies do you like best? Why?"

- Make a healthy hiking snack. Take a hike around the playground or neighborhood, but make a snack first to take along. Mix raisins, sunflower seeds, and almonds or cashews (that is, if there are no children with nut allergies) with fresh grapes and apple slices. Use a picture recipe to guide the preparation. Have the children put the mix into individual ziplock bags for travel.

- Make picture recipes. Recipes are a wonderful way to practice the beginning reading skills of left-to-right progression, sequence, symbol-word matching, and vocabulary. The best way to reinforce the literacy aspect of cooking is to make picture recipes. Use chart paper to create a poster-size recipe. List both the words for the ingredients and either a picture of them or the labels from the items. When children are reading the recipe, they can match the word-symbol to the actual ingredient. Number the steps to the recipe and draw as much of the process as possible. For example, draw a knife slicing bananas. Eventually children can "read" picture recipes for snacks and can make them independently.

- My best meal ever: Provide children with paper plates, magazine pictures, and glue sticks to create a meal with the images. Ask, "What would be in your best meal ever?" Let them share about what they would love to eat.

- Make a class pretend cookbook. Have you ever asked children how to cook something? The answers can be very funny and enlightening! Ask children to dictate a "recipe" for a favorite food such as mashed potatoes or corn on the cob. Write down their directions word-for-word, and put these together in a class book. Children can illustrate their recipes, too. Send copies of the book home for parents to enjoy.

Expanding the Understanding

- Make family-placemat kits. Families will enjoy having these homemade placemats on their tables. Send home the instructions and a piece of paper and a sheet protector for each member of the family, along with a note suggesting this as a whole-family activity. Family members can draw pictures on the paper and then slip the paper into a plastic sheet protector.

- Invite the families. One of the best ways to get family members to come to school is to feed them! After children have had a few experiences with preparing food, invite parents to come for a veggie buffet or salad bar restaurant. The children can dress up as chefs and wait staff and can help serve their families—fun for all!

- Take a hike. Talk about the importance of good nutrition when doing strenuous exercise. Help children see how it is important to have foods that support their muscles and to have plenty of water to drink. Plan a hike in the playground or the neighborhood, and bring along the snack bags, too. You might even want to find an area to "camp out" in the playground, have a pretend campfire, and sing songs!

Animals Have Needs, Too!

When children look at the needs of animals and pets, sometimes that makes it easier for the children to understand the needs of others. Perhaps this is because they see animals as having different needs from their own or because they are not challenged by an animal's needs the way they might be by another child's needs. Let's look at the needs of animals as a way to reflect on the needs of everybody on Earth!

Learning Skills

Brainstorming and discussion

Observation

Comparison

Creative thinking and expression

Role playing and dramatization

Materials

Chart paper or whiteboard

Markers

Pictures of many different kinds of animals and pets

Drawing paper

Mural paper

Magazines

Safety scissors

Glue sticks

Plastic toy animals

Pillowcase or shopping bag

Veterinarian supplies for dramatic play, such as a stethoscope, bandages, and pet bowls

Stuffed animals (optional)

Boxes and baskets

A new class pet and the items needed to care for it (optional)

Let's Get Inspired

It is important for children to broaden their perspective beyond their own needs and the needs of the family and friends. Animals and pets provide children with a means to see the similarities and differences in the needs of humans and animals.

- What do animals need? If possible, use photos of animals to help inspire the conversation. Show a photo, and ask the children what kind of animal it is. Invite them to guess what it might need. "Does it need food, water, shelter, or protection just like you?" "How is it the same as you?" "How is it different?" Record children's brainstorms on an experience chart for later reference. You can even expand the discussion by asking children to predict how the animals get what they need.

- How do animals communicate? One of the gifts we have as humans is the ability to talk and ask for what we need. Even though animals can't talk, they do communicate what they need. Ask, "How does a cat ask for something?" "How does a dog communicate? a bird? How do you know?" Collect children's ideas for a bulletin board.

- Invite a veterinarian to visit. There are few things more impressive to children than meeting a doctor who takes care of animals. If possible, invite a vet to visit and perhaps even bring an animal along to observe and discuss. Encourage the children to ask about the animal's needs for food, water, shelter, and friends! Just like people, some animals are happier when they are with others of their own kind.

- Do you have a pet? Invite the children to share about real and imaginary pets they might have. It is good to allow the imaginary pets so that children who do not have actual pets don't feel left out.

- Sing a pet song. Use the tune of "I'm A Little Teapot." You can sing for kittens, puppies, fishies, snakes—whatever! Just invite the children to help you describe the pet, and put their words in the song. For example:

    I'm a little puppy,
    Soft and round.
    Here are my front paws.
    Here is my tail.
    When I get excited
    Hear me sound:
    Woof, woof, woof, woof, woof, woof, woof!

- Should we get a class pet? Only bring this up if you are willing to take on the responsibility of a class pet. But it is important to note that pet care is a great way for children to learn about needs, feelings, and caring. Discuss what type of pet they would like to get. Mention pets that would not work (such as a bear) and ask children why that animal might not be a good idea.

Let's Go!

There are so many ways to explore the needs of animals. These activities are designed for children to look at animals and their needs from many different perspectives.

- Animals hide for safety. Animals need safety and protection just as humans do. Why would an animal need to hide? How could it do this? Talk with the children about camouflage. Provide children with toy animals to hide throughout the room in places where the animal might be the same color or texture. Send other children out to find the hiding animals!

- Tell an animal story. Children will enjoy this culmination activity. Place a collection of plastic or stuffed animals in a pillowcase or soft shopping bag. Explain that they are going to help you tell a story about animals and their needs. Reach in the bag, and take out an animal to begin the story: *Once upon a time, a little lion was walking through the jungle but he was thirsty. He walked and walked until suddenly* . . . Pass the bag to a child, have him take out another animal and continue the story with the added animal character. He will then pass the bag to another child, who takes out another animal and keeps the story going. If possible, record the story for children to listen to again and again.

- What if animals get hurt? Provide materials for children to create a veterinarian office in the dramatic play area. You can use boxes as cages and homes for the pets. Encourage the children to experiment with taking care of the animals in their new vet office. "The classroom stuffed animals are sick and hurt. How can you help?"

- What if animals could talk? What would they say? Provide children with photos of animals in interesting situations. Ask children to choose a photo to paste on drawing paper and then either dictate or "write" what they think the animal is saying in the photo! Display these in a class bulletin board and then transfer them to a class big book.

Expanding the Understanding

- Take a trip to a pet store or petting zoo, if possible. This would make an excellent extension of the learning. Ask children to predict what they will see there. Make a chart of it so you can refer to their predictions upon your return to class.

● Make a pretend aquarium. Sometimes pretend is just as good as real! If you can't have a class pet, try setting up a pretend aquarium. Start by asking children to brainstorm what might be in a real aquarium. Use a large sheet of mural paper, underwater images cut from magazines and catalogs, real shells, and recycled materials to create a one-of-a-kind habitat.

How I Live in the World— Playing and Working Together

Creativity is intelligence having fun.

—Albert Einstein (attributed)

As young children become aware of the world around them, they begin to interact through both play and work. As Fred Rogers said, "Play is the work of childhood." This is most obvious when you invite children to "play with work" and "work with play."

This theme is designed to help children notice the connections between play and work in the external world and see how that affects their internal understanding of themselves and others.

Just think about the skills children use when they play. When they play games, they learn to follow the rules and to make rules, too. When they play with costumes and identities, they are learning more about themselves and the roles they might play in the world. When they play actively outside with others, they not only build muscles but learn the challenges of working together as a team. Games give children opportunities to practice working toward a goal, coping with challenges, listening to each other, and contributing to a group effort.

Best of all, we want children to see the fun in it all. When we ask children to explore the world of work and play creatively, we demonstrate the skills that will support them as creative thinkers and problem solvers in the wide world of work that is ahead for them. Wouldn't it be wonderful if children could learn the fun of working with an attitude of creative playfulness?

These topics are intended to inspire play and exploration with our experience of the world.

- Child's play and work
- Work and play in the community
- Our family works and plays together
- Problem-solving with work and play
- Following directions in work and play
- Exploring humor in work and play
- The tools we use
- Working with energy
- Cooking with tools and energy
- Playing and working with light and shadow

It's All Child's Play and Work

Children are the masters of play. In the early years, they are learning the joy of playing alone and with others. They play with objects and without them, and they can turn anything into a play piece. People all over the world play—even some animals play. Let's focus on the many ways we play. What fun!

Learning Skills

Social interaction

Observation and comparison

Problem solving

Conflict resolution

Materials

Chart paper or whiteboard

Markers

Board games, such as Candyland

Card games, such as Go Fish

Chalk

Balls

Mats

Poster board

Magazines with photos of children

Safety scissors

Glue sticks

Clipboards

Small wheeled toys

Washable blocks

Puzzle pieces

Legos

Painting paper

Tempera paint

Sandbox or sand in a deep dishpan

Ahead of Time

Prepare recording sheets for the Toy Hunt. Make a simple chart for each child. Title it "Toy Classification." Make columns for toys with wheels, toys with cards, toys made of wood, and toys made of plastic. The children will be doing a toy assessment of the items they play with.

Let's Get Inspired

Let's celebrate playing with our friends in our circle-time gatherings. We can sing and dance and discuss the joy of play.

● Start your focus on play and friends with a simple song sung to the tune of "Here We Go 'Round the Mulberry Bush."

> *Friends, I will play with you,*
> *Sing with you, share with you.*
> *And when every day is through,*
> *I'll still be friends with you.*

Sing the first verse of the song with the children. You might consider using this as your welcome song for a while. It celebrates children and what they do together. Ask the children, "What are some of the ways we play together in our class?" "What are some of the things we play with in school?" Record their ideas in a list titled "Things We Play With." You can even divide the list into inside and outside play items. This could be a list that is added to over many days.

- Talk about problems that might happen with play. Sing the song again, but this time add the second verse, which is about issues that can arise in play.

> *Friends, I might fight with you,*
> *Cry with you, make up with you.*
> *But when every day is through,*
> *I'll still be friends with you.*

- Talk about problem solving in play. Invite the children to share some of the problems that can happen when playing with toys or each other. Children may suggest issues about sharing or feeling left out. Discuss how it feels when that happens. Ask, "What can you do if there is a problem with play?"

- Talk about games. School can be a great place to learn to play games, both inside and outside. Some are games we play with just a few children, and others are games for the entire class. Have the children brainstorm a list, "Games We Play." These could be card games, board games, or active games. This list can also be divided into inside and outside columns. If there is a clear favorite in the list, be sure to play one quick round together.

- Teach me! Sometimes a game may be suggested that others don't know. This is the perfect opportunity to invite children to help you teach the game to others!

- Revisit the lists. Throughout the study, you can ask children to "read" their lists with new eyes. For example, they might want to go through the list and mark the activities that can be done alone and those that can be done with others.

Let's Go!

With all this talk about play and games, let's do it! Focus on the joy of play while experimenting with familiar games and making up new ones.

- Go on a Toy Assessment Hunt. Give each child a toy hunt chart and a clipboard. Like workplace assessors at a construction site, their job is to look for the toys and make a tally mark in the appropriate column. Encourage them to look for toys with wheels, toys with cards, toys made of wood, and toys made of plastic. At the end of the activity, have the children share their charts with the others. How are their charts the same or different?

- Set up a toy-share center. Invite the children to bring from home a toy they are willing to share with others in the center. Only one child a day shares a toy in the center. That child stays with the toy in the center during activity time and teaches others how to play with it! In a note to families, stress the need for something safe and nonbreakable.

- Explore toy art. Get those creative juices going with toys. Provide children with paint and paper but no brushes or sponges. Children can experiment with painting with small, washable wheeled toys, balls, blocks, and puzzle pieces. Display their explorations along with children's dictation on a toy-art bulletin board.

- Create a table-game center. Card games such as Go Fish and board games such as Candyland are excellent opportunities for children to learn how to take turns, share, and follow directions. Celebrate games by creating a special center where there is a focus on a particular game each day or each week!

- Go on a toy archaeological dig! Hide some parts to a building toy or puzzle pieces in the sandbox. Encourage the children to dig for the pieces and then put them together to make something!

- Invent a game. Children love board games. Why not make one for the classroom? They can use Candyland as a model to create a path on a piece of poster board with a beginning and end. What kind of things will the players pass on the path? What obstacles might there be?

Expanding the Understanding

- Create a "toybrary." Children often grow out of toys long before the toys are worn out. Consider inviting families to send in their cast-off, good-quality toys for creating a toy library or "toybrary." Children will enjoy playing with the toys before they are borrowed by children in the class or in other classes. This is a great way for children to learn about sharing and passing it forward.

- Do parents play? Invite family members to visit the class to share about the ways they like to play. Perhaps they play sports or games or enjoy gardening or sewing. If possible, ask the family member to teach the children a bit about their favorite way to play.

- Celebrate with a field day. After exploring all these different ways we play, celebrate with a field day for children and families. Set up areas with different games to share and serve a simple snack.

Work and Play in the Community

Let's be architects of our work and play as we explore the many places and ways people do both in the community. A look at community is the first step to envisioning the play and work of others in the world. Young children develop a sense of their place in the world by exploring the many roles people fulfill in their lives. And to emphasize work as play and play as work, we put a special focus on music and movement as we celebrate the joy of working together.

Learning Skills

Social interaction

Role playing

Communication

Listening

Mapping

Creative dramatics

Materials

Poster board or whiteboard

Markers

Chart paper

Crayons

Magazines

Safety scissors

Glue sticks

Digital camera (optional)

Ahead of Time

Create song charts for some of your favorite work and play songs. Write the words on chart paper, and leave room for children to illustrate. You might choose, "I've Been Working on the Railroad," "The Wheels on the Bus," or "Heigh-Ho! It's Off to Work We Go!"

Let's Get Inspired

Singing is always a good way to get a topic going. In these circle-time activities, singing will not only get children involved but inspired.

- As the children are sitting down for circle time, jump right into singing "The Wheels on the Bus." Children will naturally join right in. Add as many verses as they can think of. Then talk about the song. "Who is working on the bus?" Children will mention the bus driver. "But who else is working?" Some children might say the mommy. "Who is playing on the bus?" Ask children to suggest other workers who might ride the bus. If there was a carpenter on the bus, what might she do? What about a baker, a teacher, or a doctor? Invite the children to think of different workers and create a verse (and movement!) for each.

- Use a work song to call children to circle. The song "Heigh-Ho! It's Off to Work We Go!" can be modified as a circle-time work song. Try these lyrics and movements. Children can add the circle time jobs to the song, too.

    > *Heigh-ho! Heigh-ho! It's off to circle we go.*
    > *With a smile and a wave and giant steps,*
    > *It's off to circle we go!*

- Who works? Talk about the different types of work that children know. They may like to start with the work in their family members do or the work they see school workers do. Make a chart of the workers as they suggest them. Ask, "Who helps you when you are sick?" "Who helps you when you are hungry?" Keep this list open for continual brainstorming over many days.

- Who are our classroom workers? We all have jobs to do in the classroom. If you don't already have a job chart, this is a good time to create one with the help of the children. Invite them to think of many jobs in the classroom. Children may like to take turns being line leader or door holder. Some children may like to water the plants or feed the class pet.

Let's Go!

- Provide children with magazines. Encourage them to cut out photos of people working and playing. Make a large chart for recording their findings. Divide the chart paper into sections with titles such as "Workers with People," "Workers with Animals," "People Making Things," "People Helping Others," "People Workers with Special Tools," and so on. As children find the photos, they can choose which column the photos belong in.

- Lay out the song charts from circle time. Encourage the children to add drawings to illustrate the work and play in the songs.

- Create an assembly line. An assembly line invites people to work together. The children can experiment with this process in several ways. For example, they could work together to make a simple cheese-and-crackers snack to share. After washing hands, some children can spread cream cheese on a cracker, the next group can place a cucumber slice on top, the next group puts a cracker on top, and the last group arranges the crackers on a plate. Let's eat! They can also work together on a simple art project that has many steps in the same way.

- Survey the school workers. What do school workers do? Small groups of children can visit a school worker and ask him to tell what he does for his job. But also ask him what he does for play! If possible, take photos of the workers to bring back to the class to create a school workers bulletin board.

- What do we need? Children love to try on different roles and jobs. Instead of providing children with everything they need to act out a job, ask them what they think they would need. This will require thinking and planning on their parts. For example, if children want to create a bakery or restaurant, you can ask, "What props do we need?" "What should we wear?" "What do you find in bakery?"

Expanding the Understanding

● Use the tune of "Here We Go Looby Loo" to create a work-and-play song. Have children stand in a circle as they sing the chorus. They can circle around as they sing. On the next verse, they can stop and act out the different work movements. Ask children to add workers and tools!

> *Here we go looby loo.*
> *Here we go looby light.*
> *Here we go looby loo,*
> *All on a Saturday night.*
> *You pick your hammer up,* (pretend to pick up hammer)
> *You pick your hammer up.*
> *You give it a bam, bam, bam* (pretend to hammer a nail)
> *And turn yourself about.* (turn around)

● Local businesses often will be open to class visits for a field trip. An important aspect of a field trip is the discussion before you go. Ask the children to predict what they think they will see on the trip. Make a list on chart paper. Then, after the visit, refer to it when you return home. Ask questions to elicit children's thinking. "Did we see everything we expected to see?" "What was a surprise?" "Why did you think we would see that?"

● Play Work Pantomime! Start by acting out a job for the children to guess. Then invite the children to act out jobs for the others to guess. You may have to whisper a job to children to get them started.

Our Family Works and Plays Together

As we explore the world of work and play, it is important to include the families. Not only can children learn about what other families do, but they can also develop a larger world view. Learning about others develops a sense of interconnection that is essential to success in the world.

Learning Skills

Sequencing

Social-emotional development

Observation

Comparison

Social-linguistic interaction

Dictating and writing

Pictorial representation

Materials

Chart paper or whiteboard

Markers

Photos from home

Glue sticks

Safety scissors

Construction paper

Drawing paper

Tempera paint

Paint paper

Easel (optional)

Family magazines

Mural paper

Household tools, such as spatulas, hammers, brushes, trowels, and so on

Your own photo album of a family event

Ahead of Time

● Invite families to send in family photos (or copies of photos) showing work and play activities they share. Explain that these will be used in a project, so they need to be able to be pasted and cut into kid-creations.

● Collect examples of household tools for children to examine and explore.

Let's Get Inspired

What is the difference between work and play? Perhaps it's all in how you look at it! For children, everything can be play when it is presented with creative open-ended activities. Let's focus on our families and what we do together.

● Share photos of your family working and playing together. Children are fascinated with your family. Perhaps it is a trip you took or a family reunion. You can tell the story about what you all had to do to get ready, to go, and to come home. Help the children see the combination of work and play entailed in a family event.

● Invite the children to tell their family story. Children can bring in an album, a photo, or a post card of a family event. Choose one or two children per day to share. Encourage them to tell you about their efforts before, during, and after the event. What was fun? What was work? What was both fun and work?

● Introduce a family song. Use the tune of "Sing a Song of Sixpence" with these new lyrics. Print the words out to send home. The children may like to teach the song to their families.

> *Sing a song of family,*
> *As happy as can be.*
> *We are all together,*
> *Working happily.*
> *When we share together,*
> *Chores and play and fun.*
> *Then we have a million smiles,*
> *To share with everyone!*

● Make a family work-and-play chart. Brainstorming time at circle! Create a chart with two columns: work and play. Invite the children to suggest ways their family plays together and ways their family works together. Leave the chart up so that it can be added to over time. Children may think of new ideas as the theme progresses. Take a photo of the chart to share with families. They will love it!

Let's Go!

You can incorporate literacy, math, and science skills in your learning center investigations of families and work.

● Make a family work mural. Children gain many social interaction skills by working on a shared art experience. Provide a large sheet of mural paper for children to create a picture of the work that goes on in the different rooms of a home. Use markers to draw the outline of a house and divide it into rooms representing a living room, a kitchen, bedrooms, and even the bathroom. Talk with children about the work that happens in each room of the house. Then hand out markers for children to draw the tasks in the different rooms. Children can also cut photos from magazines to collage in the mural. Do the activity again another day, and create a family play mural. How do the families play in each room of the house? How are the murals similar, and how are they different?

● Sort household tools. Children are always interested in tools! Set out safe tools for children to explore in your math area. Ask, "What is this used for?" "How is it used?" "Where do you use it?" Children can sort the tools in a variety of ways: by use, by size, by material composition, and/or by room of the house.

● Make a pretend-meal triptych. Focus on sequencing with a pretend cooking activity that is pasted in a long triptych of mural paper. Mealtime is one of the main ways families work and play together. Provide children with family magazines for cutting and pasting a collage of images that shows the progression of making a meal together. In the "Before" section, ask the children to show what happens before you eat a meal. "What is the first thing you need to do to prepare a meal? Go shopping!" "What is next?" "And after that?" In the "During" section, they can show families eating, foods they might eat, utensils they might use, and so on. In the "After" section, children can show the work and play that comes after a meal. Help children see the sequence from shopping, preparing and cooking the food, and setting the table to serving and eating the food. Don't forget clearing the table and washing the dishes afterward. Ask children to "read" the triptych from left to right!

● Make it a book! Children can use the photos they brought in from home to depict a story about their family and something they did together. Give the children art materials to construct their books on drawing paper, stapled together at the spine. Work with children one-on-one to elicit their dictation and write it in their book. Families will love this!

Expanding the Understanding

● Make it a song. Many children know the song "Johnny Works with One Hammer." Invite them to use creative thinking to create new verses for the song using the household tools you have been using in the theme!

> *Johnny works with one brush,*
> *One brush, one brush.*
> *Johnny works with one brush,*
> *Then he works with two!*

● Play a circle game outside. Children may like to use the tune of "The Farmer in the Dell" to create a fun family game. Best of all the "family" they create can have two mommies and daddies and whomever they want! Stand the children in a circle, and choose a child to be in the center. That child chooses a family member to join in the circle. Keep adding family members until everyone is in the circle! Sing and act out the song with these new lyrics.

> *We all have a family,*
> *We all have a family,*
> *Hi-ho and cheerio, we all have a family.*
> (Child's name) *takes a* (family member),
> (Child's name) *takes a* (family member),
> *Hi-ho and cheerio, we all have a family.*

Problem Solving with Work and Play

During play and work, children often need to engage in problem solving and decision making. There are so many places that children play and work together—from parks to schools to home. Let's look at the ways we can work together to solve both social and physical problems when they arise. These skills naturally translate to problem solving and decision making in the global community.

Learning Skills

Social interaction

Problem solving

Conflict resolution

Self-expression

Creative thinking

Brainstorming

Experimentation

Materials

Bubble solution

Dishpan

Variety of bubble blowers

Balls of different sizes and textures

Chart paper or whiteboard

Markers

Construction paper

Tissue paper

Wrapping paper

Card stock

Glue sticks

Unit blocks

Recycled materials, such as paper tubes, boxes, and cloth

Photos or video of different kinds of playgrounds

Photos of children and adults in problem situations

Digital camera (optional)

Ahead of Time

- Collect photos of challenging situations. They could be images of a child having broken something, spilled something, or made a mess. Perhaps they could be images of two children arguing over a toy or waiting for a turn on a slide or swing. Glue these on card stock for class discussion.

- Find photos or videos of different kinds of playgrounds to inspire children's block building.

- Collect a variety of items that can be used for making bubbles. Try tubes, sieves, colanders, hosiery, spatulas, wire whisks, and bubble wands.

Let's Get Inspired

This is a good time to celebrate circle time with your group. It is the place where everything starts and is the place where we can work things out—even the challenging stuff. As we work with many forms of problem solving, let's acknowledge each other and the power of the circle.

- Celebrate circle time with a song. There is no better way to celebrate a concept or activity than singing about it! Here is a wonderful song to add to your circle time repertoire. Sing it to the tune of "I've Been Working on the Railroad."

  > *The circle is the shape of friendship.*
  > *It has no beginning or end.*
  > *Everyone heard and respected*
  > *As an equal friend.*
  > *The circle holds us all together,*
  > *No one is left out.*
  > *It gives a sense of strength and friendship*
  > *And a safe place to hang out.*

- The song says that everyone is heard and respected. Why is that important? How do we help each other feel supported and equal? It might be necessary to offer examples of ways to support each other. Perhaps you can remind children about how we take turns sharing in circle. Or you can remember a time that someone helped a friend at circle time. Expand the conversation by asking, "What happens when we have problems? How do we help someone when he is upset or frightened?" Encourage children to brainstorm all the ways they help each other solve problems. Write these on chart paper or whiteboard.

- Expand the conversation about problem solving by offering an example for discussion. Some examples might be too much noise in the classroom, a ripped class book, or block buildings getting knocked down. Introduce the Five Steps to Problem Solving. On the board, write the steps one at a time. Walk the children through the steps using the chosen example.

  1. Identify the problem.

  2. Brainstorm solutions.

  3. Choose a solution to try.

  4. Test the solution.

  5. Evaluate!

Let's Go!

- Show children your collected photos of children and adults in challenging situations. Discuss what is happening in the photo. "What seems to be the problem?" "What could they do to solve the problem?" "What might happen next?" Ask the children to choose a photo to work with. Give the children a sheet of drawing paper that has been divided in half with a line. Have them glue the photo at the top section of the paper and draw what might happen next in the other half. Bring these to circle time to tell the problem-solving story.

- No scissors! Invite the children to join you at the art table for a collage activity. Show them the different types of construction, tissue, and wrapping paper available. But wait—there are no scissors. How can you make a collage without scissors? Invite children to brainstorm different ways to rip, tear, and fold the paper to make collages. Display the problem-solving projects in a no-scissors bulletin board.

- How many ways to make bubbles? There is something so magical about children and bubbles. Bubble making is another great way to work together to solve a problem. Provide children with a variety of objects that might be used to make bubbles. Show a wand-type bubble blower, and demonstrate how it works. Then show the children the other items, and ask them to predict which ones might make a good bubble blower. Ask, "What do you notice about the blower that is similar to these items?" "What is needed to make a bubble?" Record the children's findings on a chart.

- Design the perfect playground. "What would the perfect playground have in it? Why?" These are excellent problem-solving questions for children to work on together. Show the children photos or a video of excellent playgrounds with unusual ideas. Present the recycled materials they can use in conjunction with the unit blocks to design their idea of a playground utopia. If possible, take photos to create a bulletin board or book.

Expanding the Understanding

- Improve our playground. Perhaps we can't have the perfect playground, but what would improve ours? Take the children on an investigative walk around the play yard to look for things that might need fixing or improving. Perhaps they might like to have a clean-up day or put in a small, raised garden bed. You can invite parents to come to help, making it a community affair.

- Balls come in all different sizes and textures. Each moves differently when thrown and rolled. On the playground, gather the children for a brainstorming session. Show different kinds of balls, and ask the children to suggest different ways to use them. Besides rolling, throwing, and bouncing, what games do they know with balls? Write the children's ideas on chart paper and then try them out over the next few days. Which do they like best?

We Can Follow Directions

The ability to listen and follow directions is a key piece of learning how to work and play together. After introducing the concept of problem solving, it is important for children to work with this basic language and literacy skill that supports community effort and understanding. What would the world be like if everyone knew how to listen with intelligence and empathy?

Learning Skills

Receptive language

Expressive language

Listening

Spatial relationships

Communication

Body awareness

Materials

Variety of cardboard boxes

Variety of balls

Chart paper or whiteboard

Markers

Drawing paper

Glue sticks

Safety scissors

A stuffed toy

Jump rope

Oversized clothing

Hoops

Chairs

Photos of the children playing in the playground (optional)

Bean bags

Let's Get Inspired

Your circle time can be physically as well as intellectually active. This week we will explore spatial relationships and following directions with active circle-time songs and games. Traditional games such as Simon Says and fingerplays invite children to follow directions.

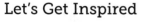

● Follow me to circle time. Start your focus on spatial relationships and following directions with a simple song. Use the tune of "Mary Had a Little Lamb" with these words.

> *Follow me to circle time,*
> *Circle time, circle time.*
> *Follow me to circle time.*
> *We're going to have some fun!*

● Change the word *follow* as you have children move with you around the room to your circle time area. Try words such as *crawl, hop, waddle,* and *skate.*

● Pass the bean bag under and over. Here is a fun game to play at the beginning of circle time. Have children stand in a circle, all facing to the right. Show a bean bag, and ask the children to pass it over their heads from one to another until it gets back to you. Then have them all turn to face the left, and ask them to pass the bean bag under their legs to the next person until it returns to you. Ask them, "What is another way to pass the bean bag?" They can pass it high and low or roll it between their legs—try some of their suggestions.

● "This Old Man" revisited: Use this favorite song but change the lyrics to represent different positions in space. For example, besides playing on my drum, this old man can play under (put hands low) or over (hold hands up high) the drum. Invite the children to add the new movements to represent the new lyrics.

> *This old man, he played one.*
> *He played knick-knack under my drum.*
> *Knick-knack paddywhack, give a dog a bone.*
> *This old man came rolling home!*

● Listen only! Children tend to follow visual directions better than verbal ones. It is important to provide children with opportunities to listen to directions carefully. In this circle game, children follow the directions you are saying but not what you are doing! It is challenging at first, but that is half the fun. You could say, for example, "Touch your nose," and actually touch your ear! At first the children will just do what you do. But the more they listen, the better they will get at the game.

Let's Go!

Many of the activities for this topic are quite active. You might want to designate an area for this exploration that will not disturb others. Try using your block area for movement games.

- Where are we? Take photos of the children playing on the play equipment outside. Post the pictures on a chart for discussion. Children love to see photos of themselves and will enjoy the photos for discussion. On the chart paper, write the words *on, up, down, in front of, in back of, in,* and *out.* Read the words with the children. These are often words children learn to recognize early. Ask the children to look at the photos to find the children who are in all these positions. Who is *on*? Who is *in*? Is anyone in more than one space, maybe *up* and *in front of*?

- Follow and lead. Children can learn to both give and follow directions with a simple jump-rope game. In this game, two children stretch out the rope in the block area. They are the leaders, and they give directions to the others. For example, they might say, "Step over the rope." Then, they might hold it up high and tell others to go under the rope. They can incorporate other movements, such as tiptoe, hop, or shuffle. Change positions and have new leaders.

- Where is our friend? Children will enjoy this simple hunting game with a stuffed friend. One child hides the toy somewhere in a designated part of the room while the others have their eyes closed. Then she gives clues that help children find it. The clue might be, "It is over something." "It is in back of something." If needed, you can demonstrate a few rounds so they get the idea of the game.

- My book of positions: Children can find images in magazines to represent the different spatial positions. Have them look for images for on, off, under, next to, between, over, on top of, and so forth. Children can glue these onto drawing paper and fold the paper to make a personal book. Ask the children to dictate a story about what is happening in their books.

Expanding the Understanding

- Children can experiment with spatial concepts and following directions outside. Bring a collection of balls, boxes, and hoops outside for fun with kinesthetic skills and experimentation with spatial concepts. Invite the children to take turns throwing or rolling the balls in, next to, between, and on top of the boxes. Have one child be the "caller" who announces (using a positional word) where the ball landed! Another day, try the balls with hoops. Which is easier—boxes or hoops? In all these activities, children will be applying problem-solving skills and will experience spatial relationships.

- Follow the clothing relay line. Here is a great way to experiment with following directions, sequencing, and spatial concepts. Set up a clothing relay in a large open space or on the playground. Put a row of a few chairs with clothing stacked on top. Have children line up across the space from the chairs. When they hear *go,* they are to run to the chair and put on one piece of clothing and run back. Those children tag the next child in line, who then runs and puts on another piece of clothing. When everyone has something on, they repeat in reverse until all the clothing is back on the chairs.

- There are so many fun games to play with balls. Invite the children to experiment with bouncing, throwing, and catching in a game of directions. Stand across from children and throw the ball to them as you say a direction such as, "Roll!" The child who catches the ball has to roll it back to you. Try a variety of movements, such as bounce or slide, and positions, such as low and high. Eventually children can take turns being the leader giving the directions!

That's Funny!

Most people agree: To thrive in this world, you need a sense of humor. Humor can get you through a tough spot in a way that problem solving might not! Young children naturally play with humor as their use of language expands. In fact, playing with language is one of the main ways that young children learn about words, sequence, rhythm, and rhyme. With a focus on the humorous words and patterns that children share with others, they can develop the joy of language and communication that bridges gaps and crosses borders.

Learning Skills

Communication

Rhyming

Alliteration

Expressive language

Dictation and writing

Listening

Materials

Mural paper

Markers and crayons

Drawing paper

Magazines

Paper bags

Small toys or objects

Small plastic or stuffed animals

Colorful cloth pillowcase or shopping bag

Chart paper or whiteboard

Jump ropes

Ahead of Time

Prepare paper bags to send home to parents for the show-and-tell riddle activity. Write or paste the instructions for the activity on the bag. Tell them they are to find a household object to place in the bag. Ask them to prepare a simple clue to help the other children guess what is inside the bag. You might give them an example such as, "This is something you use on your hair, and it has teeth!"

Let's Get Inspired

Your circle time will be filled with delightful language and rolling giggles with this focus on humor and words. It's easy to get inspired when the words are so funny!

- Start with a comical attendance song. As you welcome children to circle, use a song that invites them to make silly movements to show that they are here today. Use the tune of "If You're Happy and You Know It" with these lyrics:

    If you're here and you know it,
    Wiggle your eyebrows.
    If you're here and you know it,
    Wiggle your eyebrows.
    If you're here and you know it,
    And you really want to show it.
    If you're here and you know it,
    Wiggle your eyebrows.

- After the first verse, you can add a verse for each child. Invite the children to make their own funny movements for others to do!

- Show-and-tell riddles! Invite the children to look for a household object to bring to school. Ask them to put the object in a paper bag so no one can see it and to think of a clue (with parental help) to help the other children guess what is in the bag! You can help them, too.

An example might be, "It's blue and round, and you bounce it." The entire group can work together to guess—a great example of cooperative thinking.

- Create new silly lyrics. Let the children play with familiar songs and nursery rhymes to encourage word play as it relates to rhythm and music. This might be as simple as changing one word and letting the children create a new concept. Let children explore rhyme as they explore to the fun of absurdity. For example, you can get silly with a song like this:

  The itsy bitsy spider,
  Climbed up the cherry tree.
  Down came the rain,
  And she fell down on her knee.

- Or take "The Wheels on the Bus" and add an unexpected element. What if there were a dog, a piano, or a dinosaur on the bus? Make up a new verse.

- Write it down. A fun way to extend the learning is to write children's suggested verses on chart paper for reference. They can "read" and sing the song again and again with the new lyrics.

Let's Go!

There is a delicious connection among language, humor, and literacy. Put on your sillies for some fun language activities in your learning centers.

- Who's on the bus? In circle time, we played with "The Wheels on the Bus" song. Let's make it into an art display! Provide mural paper with the outline of an empty giant bus for children to cut out and draw pictures of all the crazy things they sang about in the bus. They may like to add even more silly objects: What if there was a pizza on the bus? an elephant? What would the new verse be? After the mural is complete, bring it to circle time so that children can sing the song with the new bus riders!

- Riddle with me. Children need practice with answering riddles before they can make them up. Set up your literacy area with a number of interesting small toys and items to use for riddle making. It is helpful for children to examine the items before you play. This will help them with guessing! Provide a colorful cloth pillowcase or shopping bag for hiding the items. Hide one of the items inside, and make up a riddle, such as, "This is something that is round and hollow and makes noise. What is it?" (Answer: a drum.) Give several examples before inviting children to choose an item and try making up a riddle for others to guess. Extend the play over time by having children find mystery items that others have not already seen.

- Tell a silly story. You can use the same objects used in the riddle activity to tell a silly story. Add a few stuffed toys or plastic animals to give the story characters. Mix them all up in the shopping bag, and invite the children to reach inside to tell a silly story with whatever they pull out. You can start by reaching inside and grabbing a character to introduce. Give it a silly name and action, and the story is off to a great start. If possible, record the story as it is told so that children can illustrate it later and make it into a book.

- Tongue-twister fun: Young children are just learning big words, and they love them, especially how they sound and feel in their mouths. Write a few simple tongue-twister words or phrases on chart paper for children to experiment with. It can be one big word, such as *supercalifragilisticexpialidocious,* or a combination of words such as *skunk, stump; knapsack straps;* and *toy boat, fruit float.* Suggest to children that they can make up their own, too—the sillier, the better! Children may like to illustrate these words to make a tongue-twister book to send home for families to play with.

Expanding the Understanding

- Knock, knock. Young children love knock-knock jokes—the more absurd, the better! You can end each day with a knock-knock jokefest. It is great fun and a wonderful way to send them home smiling. Children quickly learn the pattern, and best of all, the jokes don't have to make sense!

    > *Knock-knock.*
    > *Who's there?*
    > *Cat.*
    > *Cat who?*
    > *Under the table!*

- Jump-rope jingles are fun! The humorous chants that go with jumping rope can be fun for children to learn and embellish. Don't worry if they can't jump rope yet. Just place the rope on the ground, and have them jump over it from side to side. Try this chant to get them started:

    > *Teddy bear, teddy bear, turn around.* (turn in a circle)
    > *Teddy bear, teddy bear, touch the ground.* (squat and touch the ground)
    > *Teddy bear, teddy bear, show your shoe.* (hop on one foot)
    > *Teddy bear, teddy bear, that will do.*

- Retell a familiar story. Gather a few children around you in the literacy area to discuss a familiar story such as *The Three Little Pigs* or *Goldilocks and the Three Bears.* Invite the children to add silly parts to the story. For example, invite them to consider what would happen if there were five pigs or five bears instead of three. How would the story be different? What would they do? Start the story off in the same way, and invite the children to add to it as you go along!

Tools Help Us Work and Play

Have you ever noticed how children are fascinated with tools? They enjoy exploring everything from kitchen utensils to construction tools. While doing so, they are building important problem-solving and motor skills. Let's look at tools in our world and beyond.

Learning Skills

Problem solving

Fine motor

Observation

Sorting

Experimenting

Materials

Chart paper or whiteboard

Rubber stamps and stamp pad

Newsprint paper

A variety of tools, such as a calculator, camera, spatula, whisk, ruler, measuring cup, stapler, safety scissors, clock, hourglass, magnifying glass, hammer, wrench, trowel, sand shovel, cookie cutters, rolling pins, pen, and pencil

Catalogs and magazines

Safety scissors

Glue sticks

Drawing paper

Markers

Easel

Tempera paint

Recycled materials, such as paper tubes, sponges, and spools

Nonbreakable mirrors

Flashlights

Felt squares

Dried beans

Strong white glue

Sand and/or water table

Ahead of Time

Collect a wide variety of tools that are safe for children to handle and explore.

Let's Get Inspired

The topic of tools could go on for weeks. With so many different types of tools in the world, the possibilities for exploring are endless. Start with a focus on what tools do, and explore the many kinds together with songs, discussions, and activities

- Start with a question or two. Without showing or demonstrating a tool, ask children what they know about tools. "What does a tool do?" "What do you do with a tool?" "What tools do you know?" This is pure brainstorming, so be ready for some interesting answers!

- Begin investigating. Put your collection of tools in the center of your circle. Ask the children to sort them in any way they'd like. "Which ones do you think go together? Why?" Choose two very different tools to compare. Invite the children to notice how they are the same and how are they different. They may first notice differences in appearance. Help them to also consider differences or similarities in use. For example, a measuring cup and a ruler look very different but they both measure.

- Examine an object. Showing children an unusual object or prop can be a great way to begin a question session. You can use something familiar, such as a key, a string, or a rubber band, and invite the children to consider unfamiliar ways to use it. "How many ways can you use a key?" "What if you add a string to the key? How can you use them together?" Allow children to manipulate the objects to see all their possibilities. You can also use an unfamiliar object such as a tool from a different culture. For example, you could show the children a tortilla press and ask, "What do you think this could be? How could you use it?"

- Start with a brainstorm. Write the title "Tools" at the top of the chart paper or whiteboard. Under it, make columns that represent the places where specific types of tools are used. Categories can include home, classroom, office, construction site, and so on. Ask, "How many tools can we think of?"

- Begin with a song. The classic "This Is the Way" song is excellent for celebrating tools and their uses. Choose one of the tools you have been using, and add it to the song.

> *This is the way I push a stapler*
> *Push a stapler, push a stapler.*
> *This is the way I push a stapler*
> *To hold things together.*

Let's Go!

From art to science, children will be exploring the use of tools in the learning centers with some hands-on problem-solving activities.

- What can you do with a mirror and a flashlight? Let's work together to spread some light. Have one child hold a mirror and another shine a flashlight on it. Encourage them to work together to see how to move the light around the room. "Can you make light go around a corner? under a chair?" "What will the light shine through? a leaf? a rock? a book?" Predict and see! Note: Be sure the children know not to shine the light in anyone's eyes.

- An assembly line is one way we work with tools. We can make an assembly line to make decorative paper. Ask the children to line up on one side of the art table. Give them different ink stamps and different colors of ink. Pass a piece of paper down the line. As the paper moves down the line, each child can make a print on the paper and then pass it to the next child. Be sure to produce enough sheets for all the children in the group to take one home.

- Create an easel tool center. Put out a wide variety of recycled materials and tools instead of the usual brushes at the easel. Invite the children to brainstorm ways to use the materials and tools for painting. Encourage them to notice the different markings each item makes. Display the children's explorations on a bulletin board titled "Our Creative Painting Tools." You can even hang the tool next to the pictures created by it.

- Encourage the children to experiment with using some of the tool collection in water or the sand table. "What can you do with a comb in the sand?" "Can you use it in water, too?"

- Design a magic tool! Invite the children to draw pictures of a magic tool they imagine. Ask them to tell about it: What would this tool do? How would it work? How is it magic? Write their ideas on cards to post with their drawings.

Expanding the Understanding

- My body tools: This is a fun activity to do outside. Children can notice the ways they use their bodies as tools. Ask, for example, "What body tools do you use with a ball?" "What body tools do you use to climb? to pick flowers? to comb your hair?" Encourage them to show what their bodies can do.

- Assembly-line work and play: Let's work together to make and fill felt bean bags using assembly lines. This is a two-stage process: you can invite the children to do the first part (creating the bags) one day, then ask them to fill, close, and decorate the bags the next. Create step-by-step picture charts showing the stages of development and each person's job. How many can we make?

- Note: You can have more than one assembly line, if more than a few children are interested in this activity.

How to Make a Bean Bag

- The first child puts glue on three sides of one piece of felt.

- The second child puts a second piece of felt on top and presses.

- A third child carries the bean bag to a place where it can dry.

How to Fill, Close, and Decorate a Bean Bag

- The first child fills a bag with beans.

- A second child glues the fourth side of the bag closed.

- A third child decorates the bag.

- A fourth child inspects.

- A fifth child carries the bag to a place where the glue can dry.

- Prepare a take-home activity for youngsters to do with a family member. Make a simple form on which a family member names a job the child does at home. Underneath the job name, the family member lists the tools she uses to get the job done. Children can share their lists at circle.

Energy Helps Us Work and Play

Energy is a big topic for little minds, but you can make it simple by introducing the concept that energy is the power that makes something happen. Through hands-on explorations, children can begin to use inference skills to help them see that a toy car moves because the muscles in their hand pushed it or a doll fell because gravity pulled it. Plus, energy is an important topic for the world community. This is going to be a lot of fun!

Learning Skills

Observation

Comparison

Inference

Prediction

Experimentation

Materials

Plastic straws

Painter's tape

Large buttons

Heavy thread

Safety scissors

Small wheeled toys

Balls

Blocks

Photos of vehicles with wheels

Wagon

Blanket or quilt

Chart paper or whiteboard

Markers

Tempera paint

Ahead of Time

- Collect simple wheeled toys for exploring. Be sure you have some that do not have a power source. Others can be powered by batteries.
- Cut 2-foot lengths of heavy thread for each child.

Let's Get Inspired

Your circle time can become an energy workshop for children to begin to observe, predict, and infer the source of energy that make things happen.

- Energy makes things go. Bring in some small, wheeled toys to explore together. Invite the children to examine the different vehicles and discuss what makes them go. Help the children to notice the different sources of energy. Make a chart of the vehicles and the energy that powers them. Help children notice that some of the vehicles are powered by the muscles in their hands.

- Talk about wheels. What toys have wheels? Examine pictures or actual items such as inline skates, bikes and trikes, wagons, and scooters. Have one child sit on a quilt on the floor, and ask another child to try to pull the quilt. Now, put the child in a wagon. Is it easier to pull the child on the quilt or in the wagon? Why?

- Introduce wind energy. Pretend that it is very hot at circle time, and make a simple folded fan to create a breeze. Invite the children to discuss what the fan does. Pass the fan around for the children to feel the effect of the wind. What does it feel like on your skin? What does it do to your hair? You are moving the air with the fan, just like the wind moves things. Have you seen the wind blow leaves? Pass around a pinwheel for children to experiment with. Explain that wind can be used as a source of power. Giant windmills that are similar to the pinwheel can be used to provide power for cities and towns.

- Sing a song of wind. You can't really see the wind, but you can see how it moves things. Use the tune of "Hush Little Baby" for this simple song.

> *We see the wind*
> *When the leaves blow.*
> *We see the wind*
> *In the blowing snow.*
> *We see the wind*
> *With my kite so high.*
> *We feel the wind*
> *When I wave goodbye.*

Let's Go!

Energy test-run fun: Bring the wheeled toys from circle time to the science area. Review the energy used to make each of them move. Ask the children to predict which toy will go the farthest. They can also predict which one will go the fastest. On chart paper, write *type of vehicle, fastest,* and *farthest.* Record the types of vehicles (red hand-powered, green hand-powered, red battery-powered, and so on). Make a check mark next to the children's predictions of which vehicles will travel fastest and farthest. Using tape, mark a starting line for the children to begin their test runs. Record their findings for an inference discussion. "Why do you think this toy went the farthest?" "Which toy do you think was the fastest?"

Wheels help things go. Collect pictures and models of vehicles that have wheels. Have the children sort the pictures from a unicycle (one wheel) to a tandem truck or other vehicle with more than four wheels. Ask, "Which has the most wheels? Why do you think it needs all those wheels?"

- Art on the move: Children will enjoy using all the wheel toys to make art explorations. Put out flat pans with tempera paint for children to drive the toys through and then roll across the art paper. Ask, "What happens to your design when you add more muscle energy and push hard?"

- Put out a variety of different weights of objects and papers for children to try to blow away. First, have children explore blowing on the objects and then blowing with a paper fan and a plastic straw. "What works best? Why? Were there any items you couldn't move?"

- Make an energy toy. This is one of the simplest ways to demonstrate energy. Give each child a large button and a piece of heavy thread. Demonstrate how to put the thread through one hole of the button and out the other. Help them tie the two ends together to create a loop. Show children how to stretch the thread between their two hands and put the button at center. Ask, "What do you think will happen when I spin the button?" Spin the button until the thread is completely twisted. Then pull the hands apart and watch what happens. The button will spin! Help the children see that their muscles provide the energy to twist the thread, but the twisted thread makes the button spin!

Expanding the Understanding

- Some days children have extra energy that needs to be expressed and used. Invite children to notice how they feel when they are having a busy, excitable day. Explain that they can use that energy in a simple tightrope game. Create a pretend tightrope across the room or outside. You can draw a chalk line or use tape to create one on the floor. Invite the children to imagine that it stretched across a circus big top and they have to be very careful not to fall off as they tiptoe across it. Tightrope walkers often have partners. Ask children to find a partner and walk the rope together. "How many different ways can you move together without falling off?" Add a song you can sing to the tune of "Frère Jacques."

  > *Tightrope walker,*
  > *Tightrope walker,*
  > *Don't fall down.*
  > *Don't fall down.*
  > *Tiptoe very slowly,*
  > *Tiptoe very slowly.*
  > *Spin around.*
  > *Spin around.*

- Play a push-pull game. Children can find a partner to try this movement game. Invite the children to sit across from each other and place the palms of their hands together. First, let them try pushing toward each other. What happens? Then, let them try pulling away from each other. What happens now? Now have just one child push and/or pull. What happens? You can extend the game by giving the children a large block to move with both pushing and pulling. Which works best?

Cooking with Tools and Energy

Cooking is a deliciously fun and educational activity to enjoy with children. It is a wonderful way to learn about the importance of food in the world community. Through shared cooking activities, you help children use math, literacy, science, and self-help skills. Cooking invites children to count and measure; "read" recipes; observe change; and pour, mix, and spread. After exploring energy in general, look at the specific application of energy and tools in cooking.

Learning Skills

Observation

Comparison

Experimentation

Prediction

Inference

Measuring

Naming and labeling

Materials

Variety of cooking tools

Samples of foods, such as corn, snap peas, and carrots, or apples, bananas, and pears

Plastic spoons, knives, and forks

Paper plates

Small cutting board

Pitcher

2 cups of heavy cream

2 clear, plastic jars with tight-fitting lids

Sugar

Salt

2 clean marbles

5–6 sweet potatoes

Hand masher and/or potato ricer

Water

Herbal tea bags

Ahead of Time

Collect raw and cooked examples of similar foods that can be eaten both ways. For example, you could try vegetables such as corn, snap peas, and carrots, or fruits such as apples, bananas, and pears.

Cook some sweet potatoes for the children to try. You can make these in the school kitchen, then bring them to the class. Serve them cooled. Reserve one uncooked sweet potato for comparison.

Let's Get Inspired

A great way to introduce cooking and energy is to engage children in a discussion about food—usually a favorite topic for most children!

- Talk about food! Invite the children to talk about their favorite foods. Make an illustrated list of their suggestions. Ask them if they know how to make any of these foods. "Who can tell me how to cook one of these foods? What do you need to make it? What do you do?" Guide the children to think about any tools needed to prepare some foods. Help them also notice whether the foods need to be cooked or are eaten raw.

- What's this for? Children may be familiar with most common cooking tools but may not have seen others. Have a delightfully delicious circle discussion about the tools you have brought to show and share. Invite children to brainstorm what the tools are and how they are used.

Write children's ideas on chart paper. Are there any tools they don't recognize? Can they make up a way to use them?

Let's Go!

There are so many ways to explore the science of cooking together. Try these activities to help children make the connection between the tools and energy used in cooking and the delicious end results.

- Have a raw and cooked taste test. Help the children notice that some foods can be eaten both raw and cooked. Bring in a variety of foods to compare and taste. Ask the children to become cooking scientists to observe and compare the different foods. How does the raw food look different from the cooked? Does it taste different? On chart paper, write the names of the foods and record the children's findings in lists under each. When the activity and recording are complete, talk with the children about their findings, and ask them to make an inference about what happens to food when it is cooked.

- How is whipped cream like butter? Children will be surprised that they make both with the power of their own muscles! Have children fill two tight-lidded containers with heavy cream and a clean marble. Have them observe the cream. Ask, "What do you think will happen if we shake the jar?" Add a pinch of salt to one of the jars of cream; this will be the butter jar. Have the children watch carefully as they take turns shaking the jars. Stop shaking the whipped-cream jar after about two minutes. Open the jar, and observe how the cream has changed. Add a tiny bit of sugar, and let the children taste the whipped cream. Have the children who are shaking the butter jar continue shaking. They will notice that the texture of the cream is beginning to change and separate into soft butter. After about three or four minutes, open the jar and look inside. How has the cream changed? Taste the butter. Point out to the children that both the whipped cream and the butter are made from heavy cream—they were just shaken for different amounts of time.

- How many ways to mash a sweet potato? Show the children an uncooked sweet potato. Ask them if they have ever had mashed potato or sweet potato. Is it hard like this? Use precooked and cooled sweet potatoes cut in half. Show the children hand mashers and ricers to use to mash the potatoes. Ask, "How can we make the sweet potato soft and fluffy?" Let the children try different ways of mashing the potatoes—even their clean hands—and then taste the results. You can use the butter you made!

- Play restaurant. With all this fun with cooking, it is important to bring out the props and allow the children to create a pretend restaurant kitchen and serving area. Provide fun, safe tools for them to explore. Don't forget aprons and chef hats! Depending upon how much time you want to spend on this, it is an activity that can grow over time from a restaurant kitchen to a full restaurant with a serving area. Follow children's lead to see how detailed they want to get.

Expanding the Understanding

- How can we cook outside? With the power of the sun! Ask, "What would happen if we put some ice on a paper plate in the sun?" Children can experiment with softening or melting everything from ice cream to chocolate to cheese. Be sure to include something that will not melt, such as a slice of apple. It doesn't melt, but it does change. What happened?

- Make herbal sun tea. Children will be surprised to find that the only energy they need to make a delicious fruity iced tea is the sun! Let them place herbal tea bags inside large, clean, clear jars of water. Place the jars outside on a sunny day or near a sunny window for a few hours. Have the children watch over time to see how the water changes. You can even have children take photos of the process to record their findings. When the tea is made, let the children taste some.

Playing and Working with Light and Shadow

As children play, they often discover the amazing world of light and shadow. There is something so fun for children about experimenting with making shadows and shining light. This basic process is important throughout the world of science study and discovery.

Learning Skills

Observation

Comparison

Prediction

Inference

Artistic expression

Creative movement

Storytelling

Materials

Recorded music and player

Clothesline

White sheet

Sturdy clothespins

Bright LED light or lamp

Flashlight

Drawing paper

Black tempera paint

Squeeze bottles

Objects to use as shadow puppets, such as dolls, stuffed toys, and so on

Natural objects, such as leafy branches, twigs, and dried flowers

Digital camera (optional)

Ahead of Time

Fill clean plastic squeeze bottles with thick black tempera paint. If paint is thin, add a few drops of a good-quality liquid detergent.

Let's Get Inspired

What is it that is so fascinating about shadows? Perhaps it is the transient nature of a shadow that makes it interesting to explore. We will start in circle time with discussions and games.

- Observe light and shadow in the classroom. Ask the children to look for examples of light shining in the room. "Where do you see a shaft of light? Where is the light coming from?" Then ask them to look for shadows. "Where do you see shadows in the room?" "What do you think is creating them?" "If we move the object, will the shadow move, too?"

- Play a circle shadow game. Gather the children in your circle-time area for a shadow game. Invite one child to make slow arm and hand movements for you to copy. Demonstrate how you are the shadow and you are moving just the same way. Ask the children to turn to a partner and move together. Choose one child to make the movements and the other to copy as a shadow. Remind them to move exactly like their partner. Have the children switch roles.

- Many cultures use shadow puppets to tell stories. Put a few dolls, puppets, and other objects behind a white sheet you have stretched across your circle time area. Put a bright light in back of the sheet. Demonstrate how to make a shadow by holding up the object behind the screen but in front of the light. Tell a story using the objects. You might want to start the story off with a favorite puppet or doll. Another day, let the children create the shadows behind the sheet as you tell the story. Eventually they can tell the story, too.

- Play shadow show and tell. Invite the children to hide their show-and-tell item in a bag. When it is their turn to show, they can go behind the backlit screen and show the shadow of the item. Challenge the other children to guess what the item is. "Can you tell by the shape of its shadow?"

Let's Go!

Children will enjoy exploring light and shadow in these activities that span the areas of science, art, and literacy. How can we be light-and-shadow scientists, artists, and writers? Let's see!

- Playing with shadow and light. Bring out some interesting objects for children to create shadows with. Allow them to experiment with the flashlights to see where the light needs to be to create the shadow. Some children may like to create hand shapes for shadows, too.

- Let's make shadows move! Prop leafy tree branches, twiggy branches, flowers, and an angular human figure or other interesting shapes, near a white backdrop. Using strong flashlight illumination, create shadows from various angles and distances. Replace the backdrop with white paper, and let the children trace the shadows of one object from several angles of illumination. These can be on sequential pages or different colors (per illumination) on the same page!

- Shadow measuring. Use long pieces of yarn or ribbon for shadow measuring. Throughout the day, have children periodically measure a shadow in the room. Cut a piece of yarn the length of the shadow, and post it on a bulletin board. Then an hour later, measure again with a new piece of yarn, and post it next to the original piece. Which one is longer? Do this every hour. Ask, "What is happening to our shadow?"

- Make a shadow story. Use the inkblot technique to create interesting "shadows." Give each child a sheet of drawing paper. Ask them to fold it in half. They then open the sheet up and use squeeze bottles of black tempera paint to create a design on one half of the paper. Close the paper, press lightly, and open again. Ask, "What kind of shadow did you make? What does it remind you of?" Take dictation of the children's shadow stories and post them on the bulletin board or make them into a class shadow-story book.

Expanding the Understanding

- A sunny day on your playground area is perfect for an investigation into the way light and shadow work and play together outside. Encourage the children to walk around the area looking for places where the sunlight is shining and reflecting, as well as places where they find shadows cast by the structures. What are the differences between the light and the shadow? If possible, use a digital camera to record the light and shadow discoveries to use for a book or discussion.

- Hang a sheet on a clothesline outside on a sunny day. Encourage the children to experiment with moving their bodies in various ways in front of the sheet to form creative shadows. How can you make your shadow larger or smaller? Move closer or farther away from the sheet!

- Play a shadow freeze game outside. Bring some recorded music outside for a movement game with shadows on a sunny day. You will play some music, and as it plays, the children can dance around anyway they like—but there's one catch: Don't step on anyone's shadow! When the music stops, they should stop and freeze like a frozen shadow sculpture. Then move again when the music starts.

How I Experience the World— Everything Changes

Progress is impossible without change; and those who cannot change their minds cannot change anything.

—George Bernard Shaw, playwright

Change is an interesting topic for young children. On the one hand, they are very aware of the changes happening in their own growth and of the short-term changes in the people and world around them. And on the other hand, they are not as aware of the larger, long-term changes related to the past and future or long time spans. These activities are designed to invite children to notice change within themselves, their families, and their community, as well as larger changes in weather, season, plants, and even time. These are big concepts that children may not fully grasp at this age. However, it is important to encourage children to begin to notice change in general to prepare them for all the many changes ahead in their lifetimes.

Through activities that focus on the social-emotional, science, language, and literacy aspects of change, you will be inviting children to develop a sense of comfort with change. Experimenting with change is empowering for children. It helps them see that they can make change happen and can have an effect on the world around them. Let's start in the early years with knowledge and security with this natural aspect of life.

Ultimately, a comfort with and awareness of change is perhaps one of the greatest gifts we can give children. The following topics are designed to help children observe and interact with change.

- What is change?
- Weather changes
- Seasons
- What time is it now?
- Seeds become plants
- Changing and cooking food
- Animals grow and change
- I can make changes
- Growing up
- Past, present, future

What Is Change?

Change is best understood by creating it. When children actively effect change, they learn how change is the process of something becoming different. Let's get comfortable with it!

Learning Skills

Experimentation

Observation

Prediction

Recording

Dictation and writing

Materials

Drawing paper

Water

Scarf

Chart paper or whiteboard

Markers

Variety of sponges in different textures and sizes

Tempera paint

Sand box

Pitchers

Blocks

Small plastic bottles or jars with tight lids

Vegetable oil

Food coloring

Plastic plates

Cotton swabs

Milk

Glass jar

Small objects, such as plastic blocks, toys, or plastic counters

Ahead of Time

Cut the drawing paper into long, 3-inch-wide strips.

Let's Get Inspired

Introduce the concept of change in your circle time with discussions and experiments about making change.

- Sing a change song. Use the tune of "Row, Row, Row Your Boat" with these words for children to sing along and act out. Invite children to add verses and change movements and facial expressions.

  Change, change, change with me.
  Make yourself so small. (squat down or curl up in a ball)
  Change, change, change with me.
  Make yourself so tall. (stretch as high as you can)
  Change, change, change with me.
  Make yourself so sad. (pretend to cry)
  Change, change, change with me.
  Make yourself so glad. (smile)

- What is change? Write the word *change* on chart paper or whiteboard. Tell the children, "We just changed our movements and expressions. What does *change* mean?" "What else changes?" Don't worry if children don't know how to define the word. Ask them to show you a change instead. "What can you change? Can you show me a change?"

- Change a piece of paper. Pass out a piece of drawing paper to each child. Ask, "How can you change your piece of paper?" "How many ways can you change it?" "Can someone show me one way?" On the chart, write the word *paper*, and list all the ways children suggest they can change the paper.

- Change a scarf. It is important for children to experiment with making change with different materials. Bring in a large scarf and invite the children to suggest different ways you can change it. You can demonstrate one way by folding it. Ask, "What other ways can we change it?" Remember to put the scarf in the dramatic play area for children to continue exploring.

Let's Go!

Change is best understood by creating it. It is a wonderfully empowering feeling for children to realize that they can actually make change happen. Let's explore change in all areas of the classroom.

- Grow-and-change art: Sponges seem to grow and change when you add water. Give children long strips of paper to paint on. Provide a large assortment of sponges, both dry and wet, for children to paint with. Encourage them to experiment with dry sponges and to progress to wetter and wetter sponges. How does the wet sponge art differ from dry? What happens to the dry sponge as it gets wet with paint?

- What happens when the tide comes up over your sandcastle at the beach? Try it in the sand box and see. Encourage the children to build a big sandcastle or other structure. Don't forget the shells and stones! Then pour water to make an "ocean." Compare the dry sand with the wet sand. Ask the children, "How are they alike?" "How are they different?"

- Be a change scientist! Have your scientists use the principle that oil and water don't mix to separate colors. Provide them with several small plastic bottles (or capped test tubes, if you can get them) with roughly equal amounts of oil and water. Let the children add small amounts of food colors, one to each container. Cap, shake, and observe. What happens? What changes? What doesn't change?

- Mixing colors with soap and milk: This is always a big hit with children. Put some milk on a plate. Drop a small amount of food color into the milk. What happens? Dip a cotton swab in liquid soap. Ask the children to predict what will happen. Place the soapy swab in the middle of the color. What happens?

- Change the view. Show children how water can act as a magnifier. Give children several small objects, such as plastic blocks, small toys, or plastic counters, to inspect. Have them put a few in an empty jar. Ask, "What will happen when we add water?" Children will be surprised to find that when they look through the side of the filled jar, the objects look larger. The water is magnifying them. Children may also like to experiment with putting objects in front of and behind the jar of water. How does the object change?

- Build it. Change it. Try this cooperative change game with three or four children in your block area. Each child will start a building. At a signal, everyone moves to the next building and adds on or changes it. When they hear the signal again, they move on to the next structure. Keep going until the children return to their original buildings! Ask, "How did it change?" "How did you change the other buildings?" If possible, take photos of the originals and the changed end results!

Expanding the Understanding

- Experiment with change by mixing red, yellow, and blue playdough pieces. Most color mixing activities happen fast, almost too fast for children to see the change. Color mixing with playdough is a slow process. Choose two colors to blend. At first, they will stay separate, but as the child squeezes the playdough together, they will slowly begin to blend and change into a new color!

- Have a carnival of change! Families might like to come to school for a science fair based on some of your change experiments. Children can choose the experiments they want to share and can demonstrate them for the parents. Invite parents to bring photos of themselves when they were their child's age as a way to demonstrate how they have changed, too.

Weather Changes

Weather may be the most concrete way to demonstrate change to children. The weather is often changing, and if you teach in an area where you have all four seasons, these changes can be very specific. These activities are designed to invite children to observe, compare, predict, and quantify the changes in the weather. An understanding of weather changes helps children appreciate and grasp the weather in the world community.

Learning Skills

Observation

Comparison

Prediction

Quantification

Verbal and visual expression

Materials

Small plastic bottles with lids

Water

Glycerin

Small items to represent weather, such as plastic and sequin snowflakes for snow, blue sequins for raindrops, yellow pompoms for sun, and so on

Drawing paper

Markers

Jelly jar

Craft sticks or bamboo skewers

Natural and man-made sponges

Rubber date stamp and stamp pad

Aluminum foil

Plastic straws

Map of your country

Weather symbols

Pretend microphone

Paper thermometer

Rhythm instruments

Recordings of weather sounds (optional)

Ahead of Time

- Create nonbreakable weather jars. Find small plastic bottles with tight-fitting lids. Fill each with a mixture of 75 percent water and 25 percent glycerin. Add objects from your craft supplies to represent different weather patterns. For example, plastic and sequin snowflakes for snow, blue sequins for raindrops, yellow pompoms for sun, and so on. Children will love to shake these and talk about the weather.
- Make folded and stapled weather journals out of drawing paper.

Let's Get Inspired

Weather is already a typical part of circle time, but sometimes it can be boring and repetitive. Here are some fun elements to add to your circle-time weather discussions.

- Sing a song of weather. It is always great to start with a song. Take the tune of "Oh My Darling, Clementine" for a terrific weather song using these lyrics:

  > *What's the weather?*
  > *What's the weather?*
  > *What's the weather like today?*
  > *Who can tell us,*
  > *What's the weather?*
  > *What's the weather like today?*
  > *Is it rainy? Is it sunny?*
  > *Is it snowing out today?*
  > *Is it windy? Is it chilly?*
  > *What's the weather like today?*

- Set up a weather station in your circle-time area. Children can take turns being a forecaster! Hang a large map of your country, and provide weather symbols, pointers, pretend microphones, and a paper thermometer. Ask the forecaster, "What will the weather be today? tomorrow?" "Any storms coming?" This role-play is a fun way to get children thinking and talking about weather changes.

- Ask the children to think about and discuss what we do to prepare for changes in the weather. How does a change in the weather change what we do? For example, if the forecast says it will rain today, what do we need to do? Are there any windows open, and is there anything that has to be brought inside? If we need to dress for the rain, what do we need? Write the children's brainstorms on chart paper. Over time make lists for hot, sunny days and for snowy days.

- Play with the sounds of weather. You can use your rhythm instruments to experiment with making the sounds of weather, such as thunder or lightning, snow, rain, or wind. Pass out instruments and start the storm! If possible, find recordings of rain and storms for children to orchestrate.

- Use the weather jars you created ahead of time to discuss the different types of weather. Show a jar and invite children to predict what type of weather it represents. After circle, place the jars in your science area for further exploration.

Let's Go!

You can create a weather center with these fun and educational activities.

- Build rain gauges! Use any clear, straight-sided container—10-ounce jelly jars are a good choice. Attach bamboo skewers or craft sticks on each side of the jar by wrapping with a single strip of tape. Mark the tape in 1-inch intervals. Place the jars outside in an unobstructed space. Visit the rain gauges every time you go out to play. If there is an amount of rain inside, use a colored marker to show how much.

- Explore clouds. When the water drops in a cloud clump together, they get bigger and heavier and eventually fall as rain. Bring a collection of large natural and man-made sponges for children to experiment with creating pretend rain. Fill them up with water, and let them drip on the dolls and toys in the sand table. Pretend that there's a storm. Watch out!

- Continue water play by having children form some foil boats to float in the water table or in containers outside. Give children the plastic straws. Ask, "How can you make the boats move?" "Can you be the wind?" Children can use a soda straw to propel the boats. What would happen if a big wind came up? How can you make a wave? A big wave might upset all the boats!

- Start a weather journal. Provide a simple folded-paper journal for children to draw the weather in each day. Use a rubber date stamp to mark the date at the top of each page. Keep the journals in your writing area or by the window. Remind children to add a drawing each day for what they see outside.

Expanding the Understanding

- Look back over the daily weather journals. What interesting things do you notice? Which week had the most sunny days? Which week had the most cloudy days? Which was the best week for weather?

- Rain walk—inside! Go for a pretend walk in the rain and dance in the puddles! And, of course, if you are lucky enough to have a real rainy day, go outside to enjoy it. Note: If there is thunder or lightning, stay indoors.

- Explore wind. Make wind indicators to wear outside on the playground. Use old neckties or strips of cloth as the base. Help children tie paper steamers of differing lengths along the length of the base. Children can run around in the wind holding the indicator behind them with both hands. It is like a wind cape and will move more the more wind they can find. Ask, "What happens when you move with the wind?" "What happens when you move against it?"

What's in a Season?

In the natural progression of exploring change, we come to the topic of seasons. In the previous activities, children have studied the weather, which is inherent in understanding seasons. Now we will focus specifically on the four seasons and use our discussions to build language as well as science skills. Not all parts of the world have four seasons, but an understanding of these basic four helps children see the larger picture of weather and seasons in the world community.

Learning Skills

Observation

Comparison

Inference

Comparative language

Descriptive language

Problem solving

Materials

Chart paper or whiteboard

Markers

Photos representing nature across the seasons

Photos depicting outdoor activities in different seasons

Poster board

Safety scissors

Glue sticks

Drawing paper

Stickers

Large white paper plates

Collage materials, such as fabric, cotton balls, and cloth flowers

Ahead of Time

Prepare photos or drawings of a deciduous tree in each of the four seasons. Place these on poster board for circle-time discussion.

Let's Get Inspired

Start your circle-time discussions and activities with a focus on ways to recognize the seasons, such as a tree with blossoms, a tree in full leaf, a tree with apples, and a leafless tree.

● It is always helpful to start your circle with a song. Use the tune of "This Old Man" to sing these seasonal lyrics. Write the words for the seasons on chart paper or the whiteboard.

> *Winter, spring, summer, fall*
> *There are seasons, four in all.*
> *Weather changes—sun and rain and snow.*
> *Leaves fall down, and flowers grow.*
> *Winter, spring, summer, fall*
> *There are seasons, four in all.*
> *Look outside, and you will see*
> *Just what season it will be!*

● A deciduous tree is one of the best ways to recognize the seasons. They change so dramatically with each season. Show one of the tree images, and invite the children to guess what the season is. (Start with an easy one, such as winter.) "What season do you think this photo shows? Why do you think so? What tells you that?" Write the word for the season and place it with the photo. Show another photo, and compare it to the first one. "How is the tree different? What time of the year do you think this photo shows?"

- Play with seasonal words. Use this season poem as a starting point for descriptive language. First, discuss the words. Explain any new words such as *bowery* which means "green and leafy." Then ask the children to think of other descriptive words to add to each season. How many words can they think of?

> *Spring is showery, flowery, bowery.*
> *Summer is hoppy, croppy, poppy.*
> *Autumn is slippy. drippy, nippy.*
> *Winter is breezy, sneezy, freezy.*

Let's Go!

Use all of your learning centers as places to explore the math, science, literacy, and social aspects of the seasons.

- Invite the children to sort pictures of nature and outdoor activities according to the correct season. Ask, "Which season has the most pictures?" Children can choose pictures to glue into a class *Four Seasons* book. Ask them to dictate their favorite words to describe each season. Add these words to their book, and share it at circle time.

- Take a seasonal poll! Create a simple bar graph with pictures for each of the four seasons, and invite the children to vote for their favorite season with a smiley face sticker, picture, or stamp. Count each column to choose the "winner" of seasons.

- Create a season clock. This is an extension of the season sorting and season book. Give each child a large paper plate divided into quarters. Encourage them to cut out pictures from magazines to show the different seasons. They can glue the photos in one of the four quarters to illustrate the ever-changing circle of the seasons. They can label or color the season areas with their significant colors, such as yellow for summer, orange for fall, blue for winter, and green for spring.

- We discussed trees at circle time; now, let's turn it into an art project. Using drawing paper and construction paper, show the children how to draw a simple trunk and with bare branches on four sheets of paper. Provide collage materials such as fabric, cotton balls, cloth flowers, and stickers to decorate each of the four trees for a season. What does the tree look like in spring? What does it look like in winter?

- What season is your birthday? Make a chart to hang in your circle-time area. Divide the chart into four seasons. Use images to mark the seasons Ask children if they know which season their birthday falls in. Ask questions, such as "Is it cold outside on your birthday? Or is it very hot?" "What is the weather like?" (Be prepared with this information in case children don't remember.) Write each child's name in the section of the chart for the season of his birthday.

- Continue playing with season words. Invite children to copy some of the words from circle time and add illustrations in their seasonal journal. Have them think of other words that relate to the seasons, such as *ice, cold, wet, snow, hot, dry,* and *sunny.*

Expanding the Understanding

- How wet is it? The seasons are the perfect springboard for introducing comparative language. Discuss seasons in terms of wetness or warmth. Which season is warm? Which is warmer? Which is the warmest? Which season is wet? Which is wetter? Which is the wettest?

- What do you see in the clouds? We see clouds in all the seasons. Take a trip outside to cloud watch. Invite the children to look for shapes in the clouds. Do they tell a story? When they return inside, the children can make cloud patterns of white tempera splotches on blue paper. They can "read" the clouds and tell stories about them. "What does that cloud look like to you?"

- Rainy paintings: Well-dressed in aprons or smocks, children can drip watery tempera paint from big paintbrushes onto mural paper attached to the sidewalk. Or, try attaching the paper to the fence for some really big rain.

What Time Is It Now?

Time is not an easy concept for young children. In fact, they often mix up yesterday and tomorrow! But you can provide them with concrete experiences that show the passage of time from day to night and through the days of the week. When you tie their study of time to their own experiences, you make the concept of time come alive. An understanding of the progression of time provides children with the foundation that will eventually help them grasp the time changes throughout the world.

Learning Skills

Sequencing

Temporal relationships

Expressive and receptive vocabulary

Creative thinking and expression

Sorting and classifying

Materials

Chart paper or whiteboard

Markers

Drawing paper

Crayons

Dark blue tempera

Water

Black tempera

Quality liquid dish detergent

Paintbrushes

Paper clips

White paper plates

Sheets and blankets

Flashlights

Poster board

Brass brad

Spools

Pencils that fit inside the spools

White glue

12-inch cardboard squares

Magazines

Spoons

Craft sticks

Safety scissors

Glue sticks

Mural paper

Digital camera

Aluminum foil

Dark blue or black construction paper

Ahead of Time

Make a simple device to demonstrate yesterday, today, and tomorrow. Cut two large circles (approximately 11 inches around) out of poster board. Write the seven days of the week around the outside edge of one circle. On the other circle, cut three windows big enough to show the word of each day of the week. Line them up so that the windows fit over the words. Label the windows *Yesterday was, Today is,* and *Tomorrow will be.* Put the two wheels together and fasten them together at the center with a brass brad.

Let's Get Inspired

Your circle discussions are a perfect opportunity for children to begin to develop an understanding of the passage of time. Since circle-time activities often include the calendar, you can start introducing the concepts of *yesterday, today,* and *tomorrow.*

- *Yesterday, today,* and *tomorrow* are perhaps the most difficult time concepts for children to grasp because they are always changing. Tuesday is "today" on Tuesday, but on Wednesday it is "yesterday"! Show children the sequence wheel you have created. Talk about *today.* "What day is it today? Yes, Tuesday! Let's look at the wheel and see what tomorrow will be. Yes, Wednesday! Can you guess what day was yesterday?" Help children notice how one spin of the wheel displays the sequence of days. Use this daily with your calendar work.

- Daytime and nighttime are excellent ways to divide spans of time for children. In this discussion, focus on daytime. Write the word *daytime* on chart paper or a whiteboard. Ask, "How do you know it's daytime now? What clues do you use to know this?" Children may mention the sun, the time on the classroom clock, and the fact that they are in circle time. Write down all the daytime clues they can think of. Another day, ask them to list all the things they do during the daytime. Add these ideas to the chart over several days.

- Talk about nighttime. After exploring daytime, shift the discussion to nighttime. Ask similar questions to get the children thinking. You can start by asking them what they did last night. Discuss the things they do in the early evening when the sky is just getting dark, and then talk about what happens late at night when the moon comes out. Create a nighttime chart. Ask, "What does nighttime look like? How is it different from the day? What happens to the sky?" "What do you do in the evening? What do you do at night?" Work with this concept over several days, recording children's ideas throughout.

- It's circle time—we have to sing! Here are simple song lyrics to the tune of "Frère Jacques."

  Every week
  Every week
  Has seven days.
  Has seven days.
  Sunday, Monday, Tuesday,
  Wednesday, Thursday, Friday,
  Saturday.
  What's today?

Let's Go!

You can use your learning centers as a place to deepen the exploration into the sequence of time. Children will use science, art, and literacy skills along the way!

- Make a sundial. Sundials were some of the first "clocks" for telling the passage of time. Children can make their own sundials using spools and pencils. Demonstrate how to put a dab of glue in the middle of a piece of cardboard, place the empty spool on the glue and slip the pencil into the hole of the spool. You have a sundial!

- Invite the children to take their sundials to a sunny part of the room. Ask, "What do you notice about the pencil's shadow?" Ask them to make a dot on the cardboard to show where the tip of the shadow is. Have children revisit their sundial throughout the day, checking every few hours and marking the placement of the tip of the shadow. Ask, "What has changed?" Children will enjoy taking their sundials out to the playground, too.

- Make daytime/nighttime pictures. The art technique called crayon resist is perfect for experimenting with daytime and nighttime. Give children white drawing paper and crayons to draw a picture of something they like to do in the daytime. Encourage them to press hard with the crayons to create a good image. Talk about their pictures. "What is happening in the daytime?" Ask, "What would happen if the sun went down?" Pass out dark blue tempera thinned with water. (It should be the consistency of watercolors.) Encourage the children to brush the paint over their pictures. They may think the paint will completely cover their pictures, but the crayon will resist the paint. The paint will just darken the paper. Voilà! It is nighttime!

- Create magic nighttime pictures. Ask creative thinking questions to get things started. "Where does the night come from? What makes the night?" Invite the children to consider these questions in a creative way. There is no "right" answer—just an opportunity to imagine! Make scratchboard art to illustrate the discussions. Give the children a small square of poster board to fill in completely with crayon markings. Tell them to press very hard with the crayons and create solid lines and shapes. Then, ask them to paint over their crayon drawings with black tempera thickened with liquid dish detergent. While the paint is still a bit wet, have them use spoons or craft sticks to scrape off designs in the paint to reveal the colors below. Magic!

- Clocks don't need to have numerals. They can show the passage of time with pictures! Give children white paper plates, and help them draw vertical and horizontal lines to divide the plate into four equal sections representing four times of the day: morning, afternoon, evening, and night. Ask them to draw pictures of themselves doing activities in each of the sections. "What do you do in the morning? What do you do at night? Draw it!"

Expanding the Understanding

- What do you see in the sky at night? Yes, stars! Create your own little bit of nighttime in the classroom. Ask children to cut pieces of aluminum foil into their very own star shapes and paste these on dark construction paper. Choose a table to be the tent frame, and show the children how to tape their stars to the underside of the table. Cover the table with a blanket, get a flashlight, and go inside for some nighttime fun!

- Create a daytime/nighttime mural. Look at what people do in the daytime and nighttime. Talk about how doctors, nurses, firefighters, truck drivers, and others often work day or night. Point out that you work during the day when you teach school. Stores are often open during the day, but some are open all night. Divide a large sheet of mural paper in half. Title each half with the words *daytime* and *nighttime*. Provide children with magazines to cut photos representing the activities and places for these two times of day. This is a great long-term project to leave out for children to add.

- Children may like to mark off the days of the week with photos taken in class. Use a digital camera to take photos each day for a week. Create an "Our Week in Pictures" display by having children help you post and label the photos in the circle time area near the yesterday, today, and tomorrow wheel.

Seeds Become Plants

Growing things are a great way to explore the concept of change. Seeds are a particularly rewarding and fast way for children to experience change, combining science, math, and art into a variety of experiences they can use to explore the concept in the plant world.

Learning Skills

Observation

Comparison

Prediction

Experimentation

Pictorial representation

Sorting and classifying

Expressive language

Materials

Seed catalogs and magazines

Seeds to grow, such as bean, sunflower, marigold, corn, and so on

Sections of a tree trunk

Green cloth or scarves

Dried lima beans

Nonbreakable magnifying glasses

Potting soil

Clear plastic shoebox or aquarium

Under-bed storage box with lid

Grass seed

Fruits and vegetables, such as beans, carrots, tomatoes, oranges, peaches, watermelon, and apples

Adding-machine tape or yarn

Ahead of Time

- Prepare a section of ground for observation: Outside, cut a 6-inch square cube piece of earth. If possible, find some soil that appears to be dormant but actually contains small insects, worms, roots, and/or seeds. If you do not have access to easily cut soil, consider asking a community member to share some compost or gardening soil.

- Soak dried lima beans in water overnight. They will be ready for you to investigate what is inside a seed.

- Ask a neighbor, a local sawmill, a landscaper, or an arborist for sections of tree trunk cut into rounds.

Let's Get Inspired

With creative movement, songs and discussion, explore seeds and growing in your circle time.

- Sing a song of seeds. Use the tune of "Old MacDonald" with these fun words that children can act out as you sing.

    I will plant a garden green,
    Then I'll watch it grow.
    I'll dig some holes here in the dirt, (pretend to dig)
    In a nice, straight row.
    With a dig-dig here,
    And a dig-dig there,
    Here a dig, there a dig,
    Everywhere a dig-dig.
    I will plant a garden green,
    Then I'll watch it grow.

    I will plant a garden green,
    Then I'll watch it grow.
    In the hole I'll drop a seed, (pretend to sow seeds)
    And each seed I'll sow.
    With a drop-drop here,
    And a drop-drop there,
    Here a drop, there a drop,
    Everywhere a drop-drop.
    I will plant a garden green,
    Then I'll watch it grow.

I will plant a garden green,
Then I'll watch it grow.
I'll water each plant one by one. (pretend to water plants)
They'll sprout up in a row.
With a squirt-squirt here,
And a squirt-squirt there,
Here a squirt, there a squirt,
Everywhere a squirt-squirt.
I will plant a garden green,
Then I'll watch it grow.

- Talk about seeds and growing. Ask the children to share any experiences they have had with planting, perhaps at home or in school. Ask, "What happens when a seed grows? How does it change?" Tell them that you will explore that with lots of fun activities!

- Be a plant! Children can use green pieces of fabric or scarves to help them become a seed and a plant. Have them cuddle up in the ground with the cloths over the top of them. Then talk them through the growing process. "Start as a seed all warm in the earth, tucked safely in the ground. The sun's warmth makes you want to grow. You begin as a tiny sprout, peeking up out of the ground. Slowly grow into a plant and produce a flower. Welcome to the world, little plant!"

Let's Go!

You can turn your classroom into a seed and plant exploration area with these fun activities that help children observe change and growth.

- Create growing journals. Provide children with folded-paper booklets they can use to record their findings in the explorations. They may want to draw and or write what they see. They can also paste seeds and tiny plants in their journals as a representation of their work.

- Where do seeds come from? Set up an area for children to experiment with looking inside fruits and vegetables for seeds. Provide fruits and vegetables. Cut a few pieces of each for children, and encourage them to look at what is inside. Ask, "Do you find any seeds? How do you know they are seeds?" Have children compare the different seeds. "Are they all the same? How are they different? Draw it in your journal!"

- Look inside a seed. Ask the children, "What do you think is inside a seed? Let's open one and see!" Children will be thrilled to see the baby plant that is inside. Lima beans are the best for demonstrating this. Just soak them in water overnight. Help the children carefully pull the lima bean in two so they can see inside. Use magnifying glasses to see the tiny plant. Plant some of the whole beans to see the progression from the tiny plant inside to growing plant outside. Children can place the beans between layers of wet paper towels and watch them sprout a root. Then place them in soil to grow.

- Create a flower-picture pattern. Gardeners often plant flowers in beautiful rows. Make rows or mathematical patterns using flower pictures from catalogs or magazines. Choose a few different types of flowers and experiment with patterns such as ABAB, AABB, ABCABC, and so forth.

- What's in the earth? This is a wonderful long-term project for studying growth and change. Before class, prepare a 6-inch cube of earth to observe by cutting the cube out of the ground and placing it in a plastic shoebox or aquarium. Examine the soil, and describe what it looks like. Are there bugs or worms in the sample? How do plant roots appear? Are there rocks in the sample? Water the chunk in the box, and cover the box with plastic wrap. What happens to the earth? (Plants will grow and/or bugs will start to move!)

- Grow a lawn. Fill a clear plastic under-bed storage box halfway with moist soil. Sow grass seed, and sprinkle a bit more soil on top. Replace the cover. Put the box in a bright, warm place. Examine the contents daily. Encourage the children to record the changes they notice in their journals.

- Most plants have roots, stems, and leaves. Children can make plant prints with all the parts. Make a print pad out of a wet sponge or cloth daubed with paint—this keeps the plants from getting too messy for printing. Show the children how to gently press the plant on the sponge, then use the painted plant to make a print. Encourage them to use the different parts to create their own plant designs.

- Some plants need to grow in the protection of a greenhouse. Encourage the children to build greenhouses and other structures for growing plants in the block center. Provide fake flowers and plants, if the children would like to use them. Add plastic sheets to stretch across the blocks to make the ceiling and walls. Children may like to pretend with watering cans and trowels.

Expanding the Understanding

- Adopt a weed! Ask the children to choose a small weed (a dandelion is good) outside the room, and have them keep track of its growth. Children can use strips of adding-machine tape or yarn to measure it every few days. The tape can be decorated and posted in a row from left to right on strips of poster board. How quickly does the weed grow? If you don't have weeds, you can try forcing a fast-growing bulb, such as a narcissus, in water. Watch it grow and measure it.

- What happens when a plant does not have light? On the grass that is growing in the plastic box, place a box or bowl that will prevent light from getting to the grass. Ask the children, "What do you think will happen?" Lift the box or bowl every couple of days to see what happens. Ask, "Have you seen anything like this happen on a lawn?"

● How old is a tree? Bring in several crosscut trunk sections from trees. Each ring is a year in the life of the tree! See how some rings are wider than others. That means a year with plenty of rain. What else can we see in the tree rings? Can we count them?

Cooking and Changing Food

The natural progression from growing seeds and plants is to explore cooking and eating them. Cooking and preparing food creates many kinds of changes—many of them delicious! Focus on observing the changes we can make to our food. Food and nutrition are huge issues for the wide world that children are growing into.

Learning Skills

Observation

Comparison

Prediction

Experimentation

Expressive language

Creative expression

Materials

Raw and cooked carrots, celery, and/or broccoli

Potatoes of different sizes and colors

Eggs

Glue

Watercolors

Chart paper or whiteboard

Markers

Drawing paper

Apples and apple products, such as applesauce, apple juice, and dried apples

Raw corn and uncooked popcorn

Apple corer

Clean food-grade twine

Recycled materials and containers

Let's Get Inspired

The children can sharpen their observation and problem-solving skills as they explore the many ways to change foods!

- Sing a song of vegetables. These lyrics work well with the tune for "Do You Know the Muffin Man?"

  Do you eat your vegetables, vegetables, vegetables?
  Do you eat your vegetables, each and every day?
  Yes, we eat our vegetables, vegetables, vegetables.
  Yes, we eat our vegetables, each and every day.

- Ask the children what vegetables they like to eat and add that to the song. Sing a verse for each child.

  Mani eats her broccoli, broccoli, broccoli.
  Mani eats her broccoli, each and every day.

- Invite children to tell what vegetables they like to eat and how they like to eat them, and make a chart with children's names and favorite veggies.

- Do you eat seeds? After studying seeds, the children may not realize that besides growing them, they can eat them, too. The most popular seed for children to eat is probably popcorn! Bring in uncooked popcorn for the children to examine. Compare it with raw corn. How do they look the same and different? Write the children's observations on a chart. Ask them if they have ever made popcorn with their families. Ask, "What do you need to make popcorn? What changes it?"

- The "I'm a Little Teapot" song can be changed to fit the process of popping corn. It is a fun way for children to act out the process of changing as they embody each lyric.

  I'm a little popcorn in a pot.
  Heat me up and watch me pop.
  When I get all fat and white I'm done.
  Popping corn is lots of fun. POP!

- One potato, two potato! Bring in a collection of potatoes for children to examine. Ask, "What do you notice is the same or different about these potatoes? Can you put the potatoes in a line by increasing size—smallest to biggest?" Then play the game One Potato, Two Potato. Who is the "more"?

Let's Go!

We will begin with vegetables and also look at the amazing egg as a means for discovering the ways we can change food with cooking and preparing.

- Raw or cooked? Children don't usually think about whether their food is raw or cooked. In this exploration, children will notice the visual and taste differences between raw and cooked vegetables. Provide two vegetables, both cooked and raw, for a compare-and-contrast snack. Try carrots, celery, and/or broccoli. Talk about which way they prefer. Is it different for different vegetables?

● Bring in some raw apples of different colors and sizes for children to compare. Then share some of the many food products made with apples, such as applesauce, apple juice, and dried apples. Ask, "How are these apples the same and different? What do think happened to change the apple?" Demonstrate one way to change apples by making dried apples. Use an apple corer to carefully remove the cores. Slice the apples into thick rings for the children. Slide clean, food-grade twine through the center of the apples to make a "clothesline" of apples. Hang the line in a clean dry place to dry the apples. Check periodically to see how the apples are changing.

● How many ways can you change an egg? The possibilities are endless. Invite the children to think how a very breakable egg can be changed into a nonbreakable form just by boiling it. Make hardboiled eggs to share at snack time. Another day, experiment with scrambling eggs, if you have access to a kitchen. What tools can we use to scramble eggs? Talk about how the egg changes from its raw form to its cooked forms.

● Make an eggshell collage. Shells are one wonderful byproduct of hardboiled eggs. With all these eggs, you are bound to have quite a collection of shell pieces! Invite the children to crush the shells into small pieces and glue them on cardboard. Use watercolors to paint on the shells to create a mosaic.

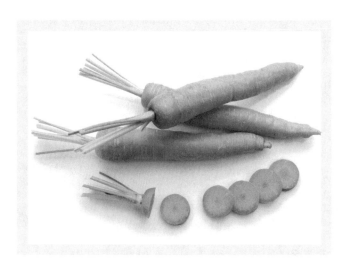

● Don't forget to mash the potatoes, too. After the children have examined the various potatoes, you can cook them and bring them in with simple mashers or ricers for the children to mash and enjoy. Talk about how the cooked potato differs from the raw potato.

Expanding the Understanding

● Have an egg drop outside. No, this isn't soup; it's a great science game. Ask the children to consider ways to cushion and protect a raw egg from breaking if it is dropped. Provide all kinds of recycled materials and containers for them to experiment with. Head outside and try dropping an egg from a few feet. Can you drop an egg without breaking it?

● Play an egg game. How many ways can you carry an egg? Depending on how brave you are and whether you are inside or outside, you can have children experiment with carrying a raw or hard-boiled egg from one place to another without breaking it. Let the children try this with their hands, a basket, a spoon, a toy truck, or other tools they think of.

- Invite a cook to visit. There is a good possibility that a family member of one of the children likes to cook. If you have access to a kitchen, invite a cook to come visit and share a simple cooking project with the children.

- Pop some seeds. Invite the children to compare popcorn before and after popping. How has it changed? Share some popcorn for snack time.

Animals Grow and Change, Too!

Baby animals are a delight for young children. It may be because they can relate to being little. Whatever the reason, animals are perfect for observing growth and change. And it is a topic that is loved around the world!

Learning Skills

Observation

Comparison

Charting and recording

Expressive language

Problem solving

Materials

Chart paper or whiteboard

Markers

Stuffed baby animals

Pillowcase or cloth shopping bag

Visiting animal (see Ahead of Time)

Photos of baby and grown animals

Sequence photos or drawings of animal growth

Poster board

Card stock

Scissors

Animal puzzles

3" x 5" cards

Glue sticks

Caterpillar to butterfly kit or brine shrimp eggs kit (optional)

Digital camera (optional)

Plastic animals

Tempera paint

Sponges

Water

Ahead of Time

- You may not be able to have a classroom pet full time, but you can borrow one! Contact families to see if they are willing to share a small animal to visit the class. Caged small animals such as guinea pigs, mice, gerbils, and lizards may be able to stay for a week or more. This will allow children a longer time to observe. Try contacting the local shelter to see if they have an animal to loan or if they are willing to come to visit with some animals.

- Print out or cut out photos of animals to create life-cycle sequence puzzles. Find pictures that represent the growth stages of animals such as a frog, a horse, a chicken, a cat, or a dog.

Let's Get Inspired

Your circle time is bound to be lively as you explore the topics of animals, growth, and change with songs, movement, and games. Children love to talk about animals!

- Sing a growing song. Introduce the topic of animals' growth and change. You can use the tune of "Oats, Peas, Beans, and Barley Grow" with these fun animal lyrics.

    Dogs, fish, birds, and kittens grow.
    Horse, frogs, deer, and pandas grow.
    Do you, do you, do you know?
    Tiny animals grow and grow!

- After children learn the song, invite them to suggest other animals to add to it. Make a list of the animals they offer on chart paper or whiteboard.

- Talk about baby animals. Now here is a topic that won't stop! Invite the children to share any experience they have had with a baby animal. Perhaps it was a pet or one they saw at a zoo. Open your circle time to these stories over the next few days so that every child has a chance to tell his story.

- Start a list of the children's names and the baby animals they tell about. Collect as many baby-animal words as you can. What is the name for a baby cat? a baby cow?

- Extend the conversation. Ask the children what differences they notice between baby and adult animals. Choose some familiar animals from the list and ask, "Has anyone seen a baby cow? a baby bird? How are they different from the adults?"

- Playing a guessing game. The only things the children can use in this game are their sense of touch and knowledge of words that describe. Place a stuffed baby animal inside a pillowcase or shopping bag. Pass the bag around, and invite the children to describe what they feel with one word. It could be *soft* or *smooth*. Write the word on a chart. Remind the children to not guess what is in the bag but to describe how it feels. After each child has had a chance to touch and suggest a word, review the list of words. Ask, "What do you think it is? It is soft and squishy and has a pointy nose and webbed feet. What baby animal does that remind you of? Yes, a duckling."

Let's Go!

Even if you can't bring animals into your classroom, you can still explore growth and change with these hands-on activities.

- Invest in an animal life-cycle project. This is one of those activities that is worth the money. For example, you can purchase sets for watching caterpillars turn into butterflies, or you can watch brine shrimp eggs, which hatch very quickly. The excitement of seeing the growth and change unfold in real life is immeasurable. Encourage the children to record what they see, and take photos, too!

- Borrow a class pet. Borrow a small pet to visit the classroom for a week, and have the children care for it. Invite them to observe the pet over the week by making drawings of their observations in a field book. "What do you notice the pet needs?" "What does it like?" "What does it do?" "Has it changed this week?"

- Paint animal footprints. You can use your classroom toy animals (not stuffed ones, though) to make animal footprint pictures. Put tempera paint on a wet sponge to make a print pad. Have the children gently press the feet into the sponge and then on the paper. Ask, "Where do you think the animal is going? Tell a story about it!" Write down their stories, and post them with the footprints.

- Put out pictures that represent the growth stages of animals such as a frog, a horse, a chicken, a cat, or a dog. Provide poster board or card stock for the children to use to create their own sequence puzzles: just born, a few weeks old, young, and fully-grown. Invite them to share their puzzles and ask friends to do them.

- Create baby and adult animal cards. Children can use photos of animals and their babies to create a set of cards to play Concentration or Go Fish. Provide index cards for children to glue the images on to make a set for each type of animal. Then play!

Expanding the Understanding

- Guide the children through movement activities that have them start as a tiny egg or baby animal. Then describe how they grow as the children act out the motions, learning how to walk, swim or slither; and eventually becoming fully grown!

- Who am I? Play an animal-charades game as a natural extension of the animal movements. Children can pretend to be an animal in baby form and slowly grow up. Can the others guess what the animal is?

I Can Make Changes

Now that children have explored change in the world around them, go back to focusing on their own abilities to make change. With the expanded worldview, children can think about the small and large changes they want to make in the world.

Learning Skills

Creative thinking and brainstorming

Problem solving

Observation

Experimentation

Expressive writing

Recording information

Vocabulary building

Materials

Chart paper or whiteboard

Mural paper

Drawing paper

Markers and crayons

House and home magazines

Safety scissors

Glue sticks

Pitchers

Water

Ice cubes

Fabric and wallpaper scraps

Sugar

Candy thermometer

Cups and bowls

Small toys

Cloth

Images of water issues around the world, such as drought, ocean warming, pollution, flooding, and so on

Ahead of Time

Collect photos that depict water issues such as drought, ocean warming, pollution, and flooding. Mount these on poster board for discussion.

Let's Get Inspired

Your discussions at circle time will grow and adapt as the children begin to see their ability to actually effect change.

- Play What's Changed? This is a great game to warm up children's observation "muscles." Place a few small toys on the floor or on a tray in front of you. Have the children look at each item and name them. Now cover the display with a cloth, and secretly remove one item. Uncover the items and ask, "What's changed? Can you guess what is different?" Try this several times, sometimes taking something away and sometimes adding something. You can also try rearranging the items for an even bigger challenge.

- It is good to change some small aspect of your classroom from time to time. Studies say that these changes build synaptic connections in the brain! Invite the children to brainstorm how they might like to change an area in the room, such as the blocks or dramatic play areas. "How can we make the center better? What would you like to add to the center? What are we finished with and can take away?" Write the children's ideas on a chart for later reference.

- Change the world around us. Help the children choose a project to work on for the community. Write their ideas on a chart, so they can later vote on which one to do. They may want to participate in making No Littering signs for the neighborhood. Or they may decide to collect money for a charity. Ask, "How can we help make good changes for the world around us?"

- We all need water. In some parts of the world, there is not enough water or the water is dirty. Invite the children to share what they know about the issues around water in the world.

Sometimes just one photo can get a discussion going; for example, show a photo of a dried-up river bed. If possible, show some images of world water issues. Engage the children in discussing what they see in the images. Websites such as http://www.kidsgoglobal.net offer ideas for talking about water and water conservation with young children.

- Be a peacemaker. Introduce the word *peacemaker*. Ask, "What do you think a peacemaker does?" Collect children's ideas on chart paper. Talk about what a peacemaker is and does. This is a perfect time to develop vocabulary words that describe the change they would like to be in the world. "What would happen if you were *kind* to others? How would the world be different? What other words describe how we can do good things for others?"

- Sing a song. Children will enjoy thinking of themselves as peacemakers with this fun song to sing and act out. You can sing it to the tune of "I'm a Little Teapot."

  > *I am a peacemaker.* (point to self)
  > *See me smile.* (smile)
  > *I'll be friends and play for a while.*
  > *I would like to help and be your friend.* (shake hands with people next to you)
  > *Let's go out and play pretend.*

Let's Go!

These activities run the gamut of topics and setting, but all of them have the focus on making either small or large changes in the world around us.

- Play What's Changed? Put out all the items you used in the circle-time game, but this time one child gets to be the "changer" and a small group of children are the "observers." Children will love the feeling of being in charge of the change!

- Change the room! Remind the children that you talked about changing a part of the classroom. Choose a center to change. Bring the children's list of ideas to that center, and invite them to suggest how to move things around to make the center even better—teamwork at its best.

- My ideal bedroom remodel! What if the children could change their rooms at home? What would their room look like? Provide drawing papers and art materials to create their ideal room. Take children's dictation about what the changes are and why they would like to make them.

- My peacemaker wishes for the world. After the circle-time discussion, the children may like to create a bulletin board of their wishes for the world. Give children a piece of paper divided into three sections. If you had three wishes for the world, what would they be? Children can draw and dictate their ideas in the three sections of the paper.

- After the discussion of water issues around the world, we need to experiment with the many ways that water changes. One issue is water absorption. In places that are too dry, the water disappears quickly. In other places where the ground it too hard, it rolls off. Provide children with pieces of cloth, vinyl, and paper wallpaper to experiment with water absorption. Children can pour or brush water on each type and see what happens. Which absorbs the water? Which does not?

Expanding the Understanding

- Sugar and water makes rocks! As a special demonstration, let's make rock candy. It is a great way to see how water can go from liquid to solid without freezing! The solution gets too hot for children to handle. Dissolve 2½ cups of sugar in 1 cup of water. Heat on a hot plate (no stirring) until it is 250 degrees on a candy thermometer. Pour the solution into a Pyrex or other heat-resistant container, and suspend a clean string with a weight at the end into the solution. As the solution cools, crystals will appear. It may take a few days or a week to complete, but it is important for children to observe long-term changes like this.

- Water can be both a liquid and a solid. Have children explore the difference between ice cubes and liquid water. Place some ice cubes in a bowl. What happens when you add water? What would happen if we added warm or hot water? This is what is happening in the Arctic seas.

Growing Up

Growing up is a powerful way to examine the changes within and around us. Children can use the growth sequence for literacy, math, and science to see a progression of change. Let's use ourselves as a focus of growth and change. Plus, growth is a way to look at the future with an understanding of the process of getting there!

Learning Skills

Observation

Comparison

Brainstorming

Creative expression

Storytelling

Left-to-right progression

Seriation

Sequencing

Materials

Drawing paper

Family magazines

Safety scissors

Glue sticks

5–6 elastic cords, each cut to 2 feet in length

Baby-to-now pictures (See Ahead of Time)

Art materials such as collage materials, markers, and crayons

Clothesline

Clothespins

Poster board

Chart paper or whiteboard

Exercise equipment, such as a balance beam, jump ropes, and large blocks

Photos of how to use the exercise equipment

Ahead of Time

- Invite families to send in photos of the children over a span of time, from birth to now. Tell the families that the children will be gluing the photos to make a chronological growth sequence. They may wish to make copies of photos to send in for this purpose. Bring in some photos of your own to show the children.

- Ask families to send in one piece of their child's clothing that no longer fits. If you wish, tell them that these clothes will be donated to people in need.

- Make accordion books ahead of time by taping pieces of drawing paper together and folding them like a fan.

- Cut the elastic cord into 2-foot lengths. Tie or sew the ends of each to create loops.

- Create a circuit-training area on the playground or in a large indoor space. Provide exercise equipment and post photos to show how to do each section of the circuit.

Let's Get Inspired

Your circle time will be filled with discussions and activities that focus on growing up and changing. From songs and movements to exercise, celebrate the magic of growth and change in the human body.

- Sing a song of babies. We all start out as babies—even teachers! Share with the children a little bit about your childhood. Show photos if you can. Add a song to describe the growth from baby to now. Use the tune of "Sing a Song of Sixpence" with these lyrics.

  Sing a song of babies tiny as can be.
  They start to grow bigger and look around to see.
  As the baby grows, he starts to crawl and walk.
  Pretty soon that baby is a toddler who can talk!

- The song suggests a few ways that babies grow and change. They are tiny then they start looking around, and eventually they crawl and walk and talk. Have children pretend to be tiny babies and do the movements as you sing to show the progression of skills. Invite the children to suggest other ways babies grow and change. Try them out!

- There are many things children can do now that they couldn't do as babies, but there are still many things they can't do. Invite the children to think about this. Ask, "Can you drive a car?" "Can you eat a peach?" "Can you cut your steak?" "Can you type?" Write the children's ideas on chart paper.

- Children are already thinking of the things they would like to do when they get older. Invite them to share their ideas, and record those on a chart. They may talk about careers, but they may also talk about a skill they would like to achieve, such as reading.

- Sometimes plans change. Share a story about a simple event that you were planning, but then your plans had to change. Perhaps it was a trip to the grocery store or a visit with a friend. Ask the children to share a story, too. "What happened to change your plans? How did that feel? What happened next?"

Let's Go!

Children will use literacy, math, and science skills in the exploration of their own growth and change.

- *My Growing-Up Foldout Story.* Gather a few children in your literacy area with the photos they brought from home. Ask them to seriate the photos in a row from the youngest photo on the left to the most recent one on the right. Give each child an accordion book to fill with their photos in sequence from youngest to oldest. It can be a wordless book that tells the story in pictures, or they can write or dictate the story they want to tell.

- It doesn't fit! Everyone has had the experience of trying on their old summer clothes and finding that they don't fit anymore. Invite families to send in a piece of clothing that no longer fits their child. Set up a clothesline for children to hang the clothes from smallest to largest. Ask them, "What happened? What changed?" Talk about how they have grown and can no longer wear these clothes. Encourage the children to pack the clothes in a box to send as donations for smaller children in need.

- Before the children donate the clothing, they may like to try them on for dress up. Put the clothing in the dramatic-play area for experimentation. Children love to pretend to be a baby again or at least a bit younger! Ask, "Does it fit you? Can we use any of the clothing for our dolls?" Let the children explore the sizes of the clothing before you donate the items.

- Collage a sequence floor puzzle. Make a giant floor puzzle depicting growth and change. Have the children cut pictures from magazines and catalogs to create a sequence of human growth from baby to old age. They can glue these in left-to-right progression on poster board. Cut the finished project into large pieces to make a giant floor puzzle. The children will love playing with it over and over again.

- What grows fast? Hair and feet! If you measured children in the beginning of the year, go back and see how they have changed. Some children grow fast in the early years, but others do not. Most children will grow out of their shoes. Have the children measure their feet and compare the measurements to a collection of shoes. Hair grows fast, too. Take a photo of each child's hair, and measure the length. Post these on a chart and revisit again in a few weeks. Ask, "Did our hair grow? Did it change? What happened?"

Extending the Understanding

- Stretching is important for growth. Give the children simple bands of elastic cord tied into a circle. These make excellent stretching bands. Have the children experiment with stretching their arms, legs, and backs. How many different ways can you stretch?

- What age am I? This is a fun pantomime game. Children can choose an age or a family member to imitate. They can pretend to be babies, mothers, fathers, teenagers, or grandparents and move like they imagine someone that age would move. Other children take turns guessing the age of the person.

- Create a circuit-training area in the playground or in a large indoor space. Exercise is a great way to represent growth and change. Place simple exercise equipment at stops around the play area. Try a balance beam, jump rope, and blocks. Post a simple photo of an exercise routine at each stop. Suggest children experiment with a different way of getting from stop to stop such as skipping, hopping, or spinning. Invite families to come and try it out, too!

Then and Now

To a young child "the old days" might mean last week. But they are ready and able to understand that the ways people do things can change over time, particularly if you present concrete examples for them to consider. Explore the ideas of *then* and *now*, not only in their lives but also in the lives of their elders.

Learning Skills

Sequencing

Temporal relationships

Observation

Comparison

Creative expression

Storytelling

Materials

Chart paper or whiteboard

Markers

Drawing paper

Crayons

Glue sticks

Soft modeling clay or playdough

Small objects, such as plastic bugs, animals, or small shells

Video recorder or smartphone

Paper cups for hot liquids with lids

Plain, large stick-on labels

Safety scissors

Craft feather

Black tempera paint

Sticks of charcoal (optional)

Dried corn cobs

Fabric scraps

Yarn

Buttons

White glue

Examples of old tools and toys

Sand buckets

Large plastic container

Water

Ahead of Time

Collect examples of old tools and toys to demonstrate how things have changed over the years. Examples might include candlesticks, a lantern, a washboard, a feather pen, and old toys.

Let's Get Inspired

There are so many wonderful conversations to be held in your circle time with this topic. Here are a few to get you started.

- Show the children your collection of old tools and toys. Ask if they know what each one is and what it does. Let them offer ideas. Ask, "Does this look like anything that we have now?" Make a chart of old and new with a listing of how the items are used or what item we now use instead.

- The children may be surprised to find out that people once used candles and lanterns for light. There was no electricity, no batteries, and no lamps. Bring in a small lantern and candlestick to demonstrate. Turn off the lights and close the curtains. Carefully light the lantern. How much light is there now? How well can the children see? How is this light source different from your classroom lights?

- People have traditionally made simple dolls out of the materials they have on hand, such as corn cobs and husks, cloth, and buttons. Make a doll to demonstrate this and show the children. Ask, "Why do you think they use these materials to make a doll? How is it different from your dolls?"

- What will the future look like? Some children may like to share their ideas of what tools, dolls, and toys will be like in the future. Ask, "What will they be like years from now? What will they be able to do?" Write children's brainstorms on chart paper for them to illustrate in activity time.

- Invite the children to remember the first days of school. Ask, "How did you feel?" Get out the photos from the beginning of the year, and encourage the children to notice how they have grown and changed. Ask, "How do you feel about school now?"

- Talk to the children about the concept of Spend, Save, Give. This is an approach that invites children to think about both saving money for the future and gifting it to others. You can demonstrate this by bringing in some change and showing the children how they can separate it into three equal piles. One to spend, one to save, and one to give.

Let's Go!

Experiment with old ways of doing things and your own "old days" of school as you look ahead to the future.

- Children will be interested in the fact that people long ago wrote with feathers dipped in ink or with sticks of charcoal. Provide drawing paper, feathers, black tempera, and/or charcoal sticks for the children to use to experiment with drawing and writing with these tools.

- Make an old-days doll. Provide corn cobs, yarn, cloth scraps, and buttons, and let the children create their own dolls.

- Make fossils. Children will enjoy pressing objects into slabs of clay or playdough to make indentations like fossils. Fossils are one way we know about life and events that happened long ago. Fossils are a way life was "recorded" before cameras. They provide a picture of animals that may no longer exist. Ask the children if they know of any animals (such as dinosaurs) that are now extinct. Try using real shells and/or plastic bugs and animals to create fossils similar to those found in nature.

- Bring the photos from circle time to your literacy area. Ask the children to sequence them from the first days of school to now. Take more photos for comparisons, and put these together for a celebratory photo album, *From Beginning to End*. Add the children's stories of the events as you put the album together.

- Make a book, *A Day in the Life of a Preschooler*. Ask, "What do we do first thing in the morning? What do we do next?" Have children record what they do all day. Ask them to draw pictures or take photos to illustrate the book. Save it as a remembrance of this year together.

- Young children often don't think about the money they get as gifts or as allowance as anything but something to spend. Talk to the children about the concept of Spend, Save, Give. This is an approach where children divide their money into three containers. Some they will spend; some they will save; and the rest they give to someone in need. Children can use cups with lids to make a collection of three banks. Have or help them write the words *spend, save,* and *give* on stick-on labels and attach them to the sides of the cups. With your help they can cut a larger opening in the top to slip their money in. Write a short note to families to explain what these cups are and to encourage the families to talk about saving, spending, and giving.

Extending the Understanding

- Children who are accustomed to fire trucks and hydrants will be amazed to find out that people once made a "bucket brigade" to put out fires. Try it outside. Collect a number of sand buckets and containers to fill with water. Have the children line up from the hose to a large container they will fill. They pass the full pails to the container and the empty ones back to get filled again. Ask, "How easy is this? How long does it take? What if there was a big fire?"

● Send a message to next year's preschoolers. Ask the children to reflect on the year. They may like to create a recording for the incoming class to tell the new children what they thought were the best things to do in preschool. Play this for families, too. They will enjoy it!

● Many people have helped the class this year, from the bus driver to the cafeteria workers to parents. Talk about all the people who have helped, and encourage the children to write thank-you notes to them. Encourage them to be grateful for a good year together.

References and Recommended Reading

Association for Childhood Education International. 2011. *Global Guidelines Assessment: An Early Childhood Care and Education Program Assessment*, 3rd edition. https://acei.org/news /acei-global-guidelines-assessment

Association for Childhood Education International. 2011. "Global Guidelines for Early Childhood Education and Care in the 21st Century." http://acei.org/global-guidelines

Center on the Developing Child. 2011. "Three Core Concepts in Early Development." Harvard University. http://developingchild.harvard.edu/resources/ three-core-concepts-in-early-development/

Dweck, Carol. 2006. *Mindset: The New Psychology of Success*. New York: Random House.

Elkind, David. 2008. "Can We Play?" *Greater Good: The Science of a Meaningful Life*. http://greater-good.berkeley.edu/article/item/can_we_play.

Elkind, David. 2007. *The Power of Play: Learning What Comes Naturally*. Philadelphia, PA: DaCapo.

Galinsky, Ellen. 2010. *Mind in the Making: The Seven Essential Life Skills Every Child Needs*. New York: HarperCollins.

North Carolina Early Childhood Foundation. 2015. "Why the First 2000 Days." *First 2000 Days*. http://first2000days.org/first-2000-days/#.VZwduEX8x90

Pink, Daniel. 2005. *A Whole New Mind: Why Right-Brainers Will Rule the Future*. New York: Berkeley Publishing Group.

Index

A

Abstract representation, 9–10
Acceptance, 52
Alliteration, 100–103
Art activities, 33–34, 46–47, 49–50, 62, 87, 89, 92, 109, 113–115, 120, 126–127, 130, 131–135, 137
Association for Childhood Education International, 7, 153
Attention spans, 12
Audio field notes, 10
Auditory discrimination, 29–32

B

Balancing skills, 44, 73, 110
Body awareness, 20, 37–44, 97–100, 106, 144–148
Books, 12, 15–17, 32, 37, 57, 58, 60, 71
Brain development, 8–9, 11, 142
Brainstorming activities, 3, 11, 68, 73, 75–82, 92–96, 105, 111, 123, 141–149

C

Change, 2–3, 6, 20, 67, 117–151
Charting activities, 9–10, 14, 36, 39, 42, 56, 67, 70, 77, 86, 88–90, 92, 81, 108–109, 126–127, 129, 136, 138–141, 149
Child-initiated experiences, 5
Circle time, 3, 11
Class pets, 79–82, 138–141
Class rules, 14, 83
Classifying skills, 2, 44–50, 72–79, 127–135
Collaborative skills, 1, 62–65, 83–115
Colors, 2, 120–121
Communication skills, 2, 7, 13, 31–34, 52, 75–79, 87–90, 97–103
    language, 13, 20–26, 31–33, 44–49, 52–60, 62–65, 75–79, 97–193, 117, 121–141
    nonverbal, 52, 60–62, 80–81
    verbal, 52, 55–60
Comparing/contrasting, 2–3, 12–15, 19–50, 69–75, 79–82, 84–87, 90–93, 105, 107–115, 121–124, 124–127, 131–151
Conflict resolution, 84–87, 93–96, 143
Construction skills, 69–72
Cooking activities, 75–79, 89, 110–113, 135–138, 144
Coordination, 41–44
    eye-hand, 26–29, 96, 98
Counting skills, 25, 41–44, 136
Creative expression, 75–82, 127–131, 135–138, 144–151
Creative movement, 26, 29, 44, 60–62, 113–115

Creative thinking, 3–4, 6, 79–82, 83–84, 87–90, 93–96, 127–131, 141–144
Critical thinking skills, 2–5, 7, 43–44, 79–82
    inductive reasoning, 1
    inferences, 107–115, 124–127
    deductive reasoning, 1, 44–50

D

Dictation, 55–58, 87, 90–93, 100–103, 118–121, 143
Discrimination skills, 2
Diversity, 6–7, 14, 34–44, 52–55, 69–72, 93
Documentation, 9
Dramatic play, 13, 52–55, 72–75, 79–82, 83, 87–90, 112, 120
Drawing, 9–10, 14, 17, 26–29, 32, 55–58, 69–72
Dweck, Carol, 11, 153

E

Elkind, David, 8, 153
Empathy, 2, 7, 12–13, 15, 34–44, 51–82
Energy, 3, 107–113, 124
Environmental awareness, 2, 12–15, 69–72, 113, 108–109, 124–127
Experimentation, 66–68, 93–96, 103–113, 118–121, 131–138, 141–144
Extrapolating skills, 32–34

F

Faces, 20, 34–37
Facing challenges, 8, 11–12, 83, 93–96
Fairness, 14
Families, 15–17, 29, 34, 42, 60, 68, 72, 78, 87, 90–93, 101, 107, 121, 138
Field trips, 15–16, 75, 81, 90
Fine motor skills, 26–29, 33–34, 41–44, 46–47, 49–50, 60–62, 87, 89, 92, 103–107, 109, 113–115, 120, 126–127, 130, 131–135, 137
First 2000 Days, 9
Focus skills, 7
Following directions, 41–44, 58–60, 97–100
Following rules, 14, 83
Friendship skills, 14, 62–65
Frustration, 12

G

Galinsky, Ellen, 7, 153
Gardening, 131–135
Global awareness, 51–52
Global education, 5–17
    making mistakes, 11

    problem solving, 12
    communicating with families, 15–17
    guidelines and philosophies, 7–8
    change in play, 8–9
    hands-on experiences, 9–10
    skills learned, 12–15
Global Guidelines Assessment, 7
Graphing activities, 9–10, 14, 25, 36, 41, 50, 74
Greater Good, 8
Gross motor skills, 1, 20, 33, 39–44, 55, 60, 60–62, 67, 72–75, 75, 78–79, 83, 87, 93, 98–100, 110, 114–115, 141–142, 146–148
Growth mindset, 11

H

Habitats, 13, 15, 52, 69–72
Hands-on learning, 6, 9–10
Health, 7, 13, 52, 72–75, 66–68
Helping others, 13, 52, 62–65, 87–90, 141–144
Humor, 16, 100–103
Hypothesizing, 66–68

I

Identifying emotions, 2, 13, 15, 49, 51–82

J

Jokes, 103
Journaling, 124, 133–134

K

Kuhl, Patricia, 8–9

L

Labeling skills, 44–50, 52–55, 110–113
Language skills, 13, 20–26, 31–33, 44–49, 52, 75–79, 117, 121–124
    comparative, 32–34, 124–127
    descriptive, 44–49, 124–127
    expressive, 52–60, 62–65, 97–103, 127–141
    receptive, 97–100, 127–131
Letters, 20, 23–26, 76
Life processes, 3, 10, 14, 38–41, 66–68, 131–135, 144–148
Light and shadow, 3, 10, 113–115, 130
Listening skills, 13, 19, 20–26, 29–32, 52–55, 58–60, 83, 87–90, 97–103
Literacy skills, 1, 9–10, 14–17, 20–26, 43, 55–58, 60–65, 78, 78, 92, 117, 126, 130, 146–147
    function of print, 20–26

Literacy skills *(continued)*
    left-to-right progression, 144–148
    reading together, 15–17
    spoken/written word correlation, 55–58
    symbols and pictures, 60–62
    symbol-word matching, 78
Locomotor movement, 41–44

M

Making connections, 7
Making mistakes, 6, 11, 16
Mapping skills, 87–90
Matching skills, 23–26, 29–34, 49, 78
Math skills, 1, 14–15, 33, 43, 92, 126, 131–135, 146–147
Measuring skills, 40, 110–113, 115, 134, 147
Meltzoff, Andrew, 8–9
Memorization skills, 16
Modeling, 8
Money skills, 150
Muscles and movement, 1, 20, 33, 39–44, 55, 60, 60–62, 67, 72–75, 75, 78–79, 83, 87, 93, 98–100, 110, 114–115, 141–142, 146–148

N

Names, 20–26, 110–113
North Carolina Early Childhood Foundation, 9, 153
Nutrition, 7, 52, 75–79, 110–113, 135–138

O

Object permanence, 47
Observation skills, 2–3, 12–14, 19–50, 66–75, 79–82, 84–87, 90–93, 103–115, 118–127, 131–151
Open-ended learning, 5–17
Opposites, 20, 32–34
Outdoor play, 22–23, 28–29, 32, 34, 39, 41, 44, 46–47, 55, 60, 62, 65, 68, 72, 75, 78–79, 83, 86–87, 93, 96, 99, 110, 113, 115, 124, 127, 137, 147–148

P

Patterns, 134
Perception, 1, 3, 19–50
Perseverance, 12
Personal hygiene, 13
Perspective taking, 1, 3, 6, 8, 19–50, 79–82
Piaget, Jean, 10
Pictorial representation, 90–93, 131–135
Pink, Daniel, 6, 153
Play-based learning, 8–9, 83–115
Predicting skills, 10, 14–15, 44–50, 72–75, 81, 107–115, 118–124, 131–138
Prepositional concepts, 13
Problem solving skills, 2–3, 7, 11–12, 14, 43–50, 69–75, 84–87, 93–96, 103–107, 124–127, 138–144
Puppets, 54, 58–60, 113–115
Puzzles, 85, 138, 147

Q

Quantification, 121–124
Questioning skills, 2, 4, 11, 16, 130

R

Reading together, 15–17
Receptive language, 97–100, 127–131
Recorded music, 29, 31, 55, 113, 115
Recording data, 9–10, 14, 66–68, 118–121, 138–144
Relationships, 1–3, 13
Representational function, 9–10, 14
Rhyming, 100–103, 125–126
Rhythm, 100
    instruments, 122
Riddles, 101–102
Risk taking, 11–12
Rogers, Fred, 83
Role awareness, 52–55
Role playing, 13, 52–55, 58–60, 79–82, 87–90

S

Safety, 14, 52, 72–75
Science activities, 1–3, 10, 14–15, 33, 43, 46, 49–50, 66–68, 92, 107–115, 117, 120, 126, 130–135, 146–147
Seasons, 14, 124–127
Security, 6–7, 11–12
Self-awareness, 23–26, 34–44, 52
Self-control, 3, 7, 12, 62–65
Self-directed learning, 8
Self-esteem, 20–26
Self-expression, 93–96
Self-image, 12–13
Self-reflection, 69–72
Sensory motor skills, 2, 9–10, 12, 20, 28–32, 44–50
Sequencing skills, 13–15, 17, 58–60, 78, 90–93, 100, 115, 127–131, 138–141, 144–151
Seriation, 144–148
Shapes, 2, 38, 47
Sharing, 14, 86
Shonkoff, Jack, 9
Singing activities, 3, 21, 25–26, 28, 30, 32–34, 40, 42, 46, 48, 56, 59, 61, 64, 67, 70, 73–74, 76–77, 79–80, 85–86, 88, 90, 92–93, 95, 98, 101–102, 105, 109–110, 119, 122, 125, 129, 132–133, 136, 139, 143, 146
Sizes, 2, 47
Snack time, 26, 75–79, 89, 110–113, 135–138, 144
Social interaction, 58–60, 62–65, 84–90, 93–96
Social-emotional development, 1–2, 12, 14, 34–44, 52–55, 90–93, 117, 126
    empathy, 2, 7, 12–13, 15, 34–44, 51–82
    friendship skills, 14, 62–65
    identifying emotions, 2, 13, 15, 49, 51–82

Social-linguistic interaction, 90–93
Songs
    "A Tisket, A Tasket," 56–57
    "A, A, A It Is," 25
    "Change, Change, Change With Me," 119
    "The Circle Is the Shape of Friendship," 95
    "Did You Ever Hear a Drum Beat?" 30
    "Do You Eat Your Vegetables?" 136
    "Dogs, Fish, Birds, and Kittens Grow," 139
    "Every Week," 129
    "The Farmer in the Dell," 25–26
    "Follow Me to Circle Time," 98
    "The Friend in the Middle," 64
    "Friends, I Will Play With You," 85–86
    "Head, Shoulders, Knees, and Toes," 44
    "Heigh-Ho!" 88
    "Here We Go Looby Loo," 90
    "The Hokey Pokey," 44
    "H-O-U-S-E," 70
    "I Am a Peacemaker," 143
    "I Need You," 76–77
    "I Use My Eyes to See," 48
    "I Will Plant a Garden Green," 132–133
    "I'm a Little Popcorn," 136
    "I'm a Little Puppy," 80
    "I've Been Working on the Railroad," 88
    "If You're Happy and You Know It," 42, 101
    "The Itsy Bitsy Spider," 102
    "Johnny Works With One Brush," 93
    "Keep Healthy," 74
    "Listen, Children," 28
    "My Fingers Are Starting to Wiggle," 42
    "My Hand Says Hello," 61
    "The Noble Duke of York," 34
    "Sing a Song of Babies," 146
    "Sing a Song of Family," 92
    "Sing a Song of Seeing," 46
    "Skip to My Lou," 44
    "This Is the Way," 105
    "This Is the Way," 73
    "This Old Man," 98
    "Three Little Fishies," 67
    "Tightrope Walker," 110
    "We All Have a Family," 93
    "We See the Wind," 109
    "What's the Weather?" 122
    "The Wheels on the Bus," 88, 102
    "Where, Oh Where Is Our Friend?" 21
    "Whoever Has Brown Hair," 40
    "Winter, Spring, Summer, Fall," 125
Sorting skills, 39, 44–50, 72–79, 92, 103–107, 109, 126–135
Sounds, 20, 29–32

Spatial concepts, 13, 58–60, 97–100
Spoken/written word correlation, 55–58
Storytelling, 14–17, 58–62, 68, 81, 91, 93,
     102–103, 113–115, 140, 144–151
Symbolic function, 10
Symbol-word matching, 78
Symmetry, 37

T
Taking turns, 24
Tallying skills, 41–44
Teacher's role, 8–9
Technology, 8–10

Temperature, 49–50
Temporal relationships, 127–131, 148–151
Then and now, 148–151
Time awareness, 14, 127–131, 148–151
Tongue twisters, 102–103
Tools, 2–3, 14, 72, 91, 103–107, 110–113,
     149
Triptychs, 92–93

V
Venn diagrams, 33–34
Vision, 20, 44–47
Visual discrimination, 23–26

Visual expression, 121–124
Vocabulary, 78, 126–131, 141–144

W
Work awareness, 3, 14, 83–115
Working together, 83–115
Writing skills, 15–17, 20, 26–29, 52–58,
     64–65, 68–72, 75–79, 90–93, 100–
     103, 118–121, 141–144]